THE
BEST
PUBLIC
SPEAKING
BOOK

For instructional videos and other public speaking resources, please visit

www.BestPublicSpeakingBook.com

And for information on Dr. Deaton's various projects and products

www.MattDeaton.com

THE BEST PUBLIC SPEAKING BOOK

How to Conquer Nervousness,
Polish Your Authentic Stage Self,
Develop & Deliver
Dynamite Presentations

MATT DEATON, PH.D.

The Best Public Speaking Book
How to Conquer Nervousness, Polish Your Authentic Stage Self,
Develop & Deliver Dynamite Presentations

Published by Notaed Press, Hanover, MD

ISBN 978-0-9892542-0-5

Cover Image by Tonya Cinnamon of Cinnamon Studios

Copyediting by Hayley Shepherd of Miss Pelt's Literacy Services

General editorial consultation by Roberta Israeloff and Melody Gonzales

Proofing by Alexandra P. Chiasson

Interior design by John Richard Stephens

For my students:

past, present and future.

CONTENTS

13 Tell Them What You've Told Them 165

Chapter One

WELCOME!

Hi—I'm Matt Deaton, your new public speaking coach. Please call me Matt.

Once a clumsy, stage-frightened rookie, I know firsthand how intimidating public speaking can be. And for a long time, I avoided it at all costs.

But in just a few short years, I graduated from inexperienced novice to university lecturer, stand-up comedian and live television host. I no longer avoid public speaking—I actively seek it out. And when I'm lucky enough to do it, I savor every moment.

I've presented on hundreds of occasions and to thousands of people. Below you'll find the streamlined keys to success I've learned along the way. And I know for a fact the method in this book works, for I've already used its core to successfully coach hundreds of aspiring speakers just like you.

I'm confident this book will work for you in particular because you possess the two traits necessary to succeed: the courage to get up there and the commitment to get better. For if you didn't have at least a little courage and some commitment, you wouldn't be reading these words.

So you bring a seed of courage and a pinch of commitment, and I'll bring the know-how and encouragement. Deal?

Together we'll develop your skill and bolster your confidence until you're so comfortable and so effective on stage that you not only survive presentations, but thrive as a public speaker, and like me, actively seek out opportunities to do it more. The less experience you have, the more exciting, rewarding and fun this journey is going to be—for both of us.

THE NOT-SO-SECRET SECRET

First, you need to recognize the not-so-secret secret of public speaking. And that not-so-secret secret is that growth requires practice.

You can read books about swimming, know all the technical aspects of the strokes, and even practice them on land. But until you actually get in the water, you are not a swimmer, nor will you get any better at swimming. To experience the joy of swimming, and the confidence and satisfaction of knowing how to swim, sooner or later, you simply have to jump in.

The same is true for public speaking. You can read, study, simulate and reflect. But without actual stage time, there's a limit to how much you can improve.

That's why a large part of this book is motivation. We need you in front of an audience—any audience—as soon and as often as possible. So apart from teaching you exactly how to develop and deliver dynamite presentations, and providing an explicit and customizable action plan, I'm going to nudge and encourage you dozens of times in dozens of ways. That's what coaches do. So get used to it!

THE TIME IS NOW

People who wait for the perfect moment to go back to school, get married, or start their dream business wait until they're dead. That's why one difference between successful and unsuccessful people is that successful people consistently act before they feel fully prepared. While it's wise to think before you act, this year is better than next year. Today is better than tomorrow. Now is better than later.

If you wait until you feel completely prepared to give your first or your next presentation, that moment will never come. I put it off for years, largely because I was scared, thought there was too much to learn, and believed I'd never be good enough. Seeing those experts on television whom I thought I could never match, and not knowing where to begin, the challenge just appeared too big—especially after making it into adulthood with very little speaking experience. "I've made it this far," I thought. "No reason to invite all that heartache into my life now."

Little did I know how much happier I'd be, and how many doors would open once I could present any idea to any crowd, anywhere, anytime. Contrary to what I had imagined, the basic formula was surprisingly simple.

PUBLIC SPEAKING SIMPLIFIED: COMMUNICATION

Public speaking is communication. That's it. You have ideas in your head you'd like to transfer into the heads of your audience members. Accomplish that basic task of idea transfer via spoken language and you're a public speaking success.

Public speaking is a *special kind* of communication, with special conventions, expectations, challenges and opportunities. But don't let anyone—including me—make it more complex than it really is. Remember now and forever: public speaking is communication. That's it.

Doing it especially well—comfortably, competently, with poise, grace, effectiveness and pleasure—takes a little knowledge and practice. But you've come to the right place for both.

TELL THEM WHAT YOU'RE ABOUT TO TELL THEM

If you're anything like I used to be, even reading about public speaking makes you a little antsy. That's why we'll pinpoint the underlying causes of public speaking nervousness and focus on taking actions that minimize your self-consciousness and maximize your self-confidence first thing. We'll cover tips on mindset, posture, and wardrobe, and even work through a drill borrowed from the world of self-defense that's designed to boost your confidence and assertiveness in a hurry.

In Chapter Three we'll tackle message development. You'll learn to create, organize and revise your presentations in a way that will make them easy to deliver, easy to understand, and more likely to stick. You'll learn how to arrange your points in a logical order, deepen your audience's understanding with analogies, illustrations, examples, and callbacks, and how to transform that initial spark into a fully polished presentation using an intuitive seven-step method.

In Chapters Four and Five we'll dive into the technical aspects of physical and then oral delivery. You'll learn how to tailor your silent message and carry yourself in a way that will instantly win your audience's respect, how enunciation and voice projection are essential to your audience's understanding, as well as when to use—and when *not* to use—a lectern.

Welcome!

In Chapter Six you'll learn the keys to properly using a script on the rare occasion that doing so is appropriate. And in Chapter Seven you'll learn how to capture and hold your audience's attention by engaging their minds, and in some cases, their bodies.

In Chapter Eight you'll learn how to seamlessly incorporate technology—how to use PowerPoint as an illustrative aid rather than a distracting crutch, how to effectively present over speakerphone or webcam, and even how to properly handle a microphone.

Then in Chapter Nine: *Less Reading, More Doing,* I'll push you to customize and deliver a series of confidence and experience-building practice presentations that start out simple, and slowly progress in terms of both stakes and complexity. We'll work our way from a simple personal introduction, all the way through the presentation you envisioned yourself delivering when you picked up this book. And then I'll encourage you to dream even bigger.

In Chapter Ten I'll teach you how to grow from every speaking opportunity, using two recent presentations of my own as examples. I'll teach you how to carefully analyze your performances so you can build on your strengths and effectively address your opportunities for improvement, such that each and every opportunity to speak adds some value.

In Chapter Eleven you'll learn the importance of being true to your genuine self as a speaker—how and why to "Do You," as Russell Simmons likes to say.

In Chapter Twelve you'll learn how to overcome the evil of perfectionism, how to rid yourself of subconscious sabotage, and how to view challenges as opportunities and setbacks as invaluable chances to learn.

Last, in Chapter Thirteen we'll glean some parting wisdom from some people who know a thing or two about courage, growth and perseverance, and reflect on all you've learned before closing.

With every word, keep in mind that not-so-secret secret: *to improve you must practice.*

Key Takeaways

- ⊃ Public speaking is **communication**—simple idea transfer

- ⊃ Improving as a speaker takes two things: the **courage** to get up there and the **commitment** to get better—you have both

- ⊃ Successful people **act** before they're fully ready—so let's begin!

Chapter Two

CONQUERING
NERVOUSNESS

Every public speaker gets nervous. Even seasoned politicians, professional actors and news anchors get butterflies from time to time. Why?

Speaking comfort seems to be a function of a presenter's perceived likelihood of success and perceived importance of the stakes. That is, a public speaker is likely to feel comfortable and in control to the extent that he is sure of himself, his abilities and his message, and to the extent that he believes the implications of his talk are unimportant and secure.

On the other hand, a public speaker is likely to be nervous to the extent that he is unsure of himself, his speaking abilities and his message, and to the extent that he believes the implications of his talk are important and at risk.

This is true for many things in life. As our perceived ability to perform goes up and the stakes go down, we're more likely to feel confident and in control. And as our perceived ability to perform goes down and the stakes go up, we're more likely to feel nervous.

→ Fully prepared & no big deal = confident
→ Not prepared & really big deal = nervous

Consider two drivers caught in the same snowstorm. One is a native Alaskan taking a leisurely trip to the market. The other is a native Hawaiian—seeing snow for the first time—rushing his pregnant wife to the hospital.

Obviously the Hawaiian is much less prepared and has much more on the line than the Alaskan, so we can expect him to be very nervous, at least in comparison to the Alaskan. But regardless of his mental state, the important question is: what should he do?

FOCUS WHERE IT MATTERS— ACT WHERE IT COUNTS

Beyond turning on his emergency flashers, focusing on the road, and perhaps praying, there's not much the Hawaiian caught in the snowstorm *can* do. Fretting over what might go wrong (What if the gas line freezes? What if this snow turns to ice? What if the Abominable Snowman mistakes my car for a reindeer and eats it?!) is worse than useless—it's harmful.

As Stephen Covey, author of *The Seven Habits of Highly Effective People* puts it, a wise person aligns his or her "Circle of Concern" with his or her "Circle of Influence." That is, few things are more frustrating and pointless than fixating on problems we lack the power to control. But few things are more satisfying and productive than taking immediate action to achieve goals within our power.

This nugget of wisdom is expressed succinctly in the world-famous Serenity Prayer, attributed to twentieth century American theologian, Reinhold Niebuhr:

> God, grant me the serenity to accept the things I cannot change, the courage to change the things I can, and the wisdom to know the difference.

Whether you accept, tolerate or simply ignore the things you cannot change is up to you. Just remember, as author and life coach Byron Katie says, "When you argue with reality, you lose...but only 100% of the time."

As public speakers, we'll seldom be able to influence whether our audience arrives enthused, energized and receptive, or depressed, tired, and...*blah*. We usually won't be able to control what's at stake either, be it a promotion at work, a grade for a class, or the simple admiration of our audience.

So resist the temptation to amplify worries beyond your control, and direct your energy at whatever will do the most to achieve your goals. In a phrase: *Focus where it matters and act where it counts.* In an acronym: *FM-AC.* Just like a car isn't fully functioning unless it has an FM radio and AC (air conditioning), we aren't complete until we're Focusing where it Matters and Acting where it Counts. In both cases, the key is FM-AC.

Deciding to FM-AC ensures your time and energy are wisely spent. We may be unable to control the stakes or our audience's attitude, but we can certainly control how well we prepare. And when it comes to preparation, few things will more dramatically impact your effectiveness than how well you understand your material.

KNOW THY MATERIAL

Whether you're talking about widget fasteners, batting averages, deficit spending, or rocket boosters; whether you're delivering a speech to an auditorium or just deliberating with colleagues—knowing what you're talking about is an absolutely vital key to effective public speaking.

Why is this the case? When you know what you're talking about, everything—and I mean *everything*—improves. When you don't know what you're talking about, everything—and I mean *everything*—gets worse.

Back in my philosophy professor days, whenever I'd take the time to study, organize, and internalize my lesson plan, I could illustrate points with impromptu examples, diagram interconnected concepts on the board, and answer tough questions with ease. However, on days when I threw my presentation together at the last minute—even when I thought I understood the ideas—I'd struggle to articulate my points, stumble through crude explanations, and worry the whole time a student would ask a question I couldn't answer.

That's why knowing your material is so important. Not only does it impact the content of your presentation, but also the quality of your delivery. On the days I knew my stuff, and *knew* I knew my stuff, the confidence that naturally followed felt great! But on days I didn't know my stuff, and *knew* I didn't know my stuff, the anxiety that naturally followed made me feel terrible. One third of the class would look confused, one third would look frustrated, and the other third would look out the window.

Of course, proper preparation takes time and effort. But it's oh so worth it. If you can't master your subject matter, at least figure it out the best you can given your resources, for few things will do more to improve your effectiveness as a speaker.

RELEASE THE NEGATIVE & AMPLIFY THE POSITIVE

"I always mess up—I'll never be any good," my four-year-old said in disgust, walking off the soccer field after an especially frustrating practice. A teammate, only a year older, immediately interrupted: "Don't say that. One time I said I wasn't any good at baseball. But I practiced and got better."

Now there's a leader in the making. To recognize that a defeatist mindset is not only counterproductive, but irrational, and to have the goodwill and courage to coach a teammate in need—*at five?* Let's just say I made a point to tell his parents, and they had every reason to be very proud.

Thanks to a thoughtful and exceptionally mature team-mate, my son's attitude changed almost overnight. He went from seeing himself as a soccer flunky who would never im-prove, to a rising star on a winding path to greatness, and his performance improved almost immediately.

In the grand scheme of things, how good a person is at soccer, especially when they're four, is pretty insignificant. But the lesson at the heart of this story is very significant. When it comes to skill and performance, we're rarely any bet-ter than we believe.

Take this example: "I'm terrible with names." We've all heard someone say this—inevitably someone indeed terrible with names. But as Susan RoAne explains in *How to Work a Room*, to be good at remembering names, you must first stop repeating that you're bad at remembering names. Then all it takes is creative association and repetition.

Meeting a man named John? As you shake hands, look in-to his eyes, and visualize him in the "john" shaving. Or imagine him reading a "Dear John" letter, or signing his John Hancock. Or combine all three: imagine John in the john, having just read a heartbreaking "Dear John" letter, consoling himself by repeatedly signing his John Hancock on the walls.

Meeting a group of people? Do the association trick for each, internally quiz yourself (so it's Sally, Fred, and crazy bathroom John), and confirm you have it right as they depart. Should you forget someone's name, admit it, remind them of *your* name, and run the same drill again.

The point is that remembering names is easy. But if you're stuck at "I'm terrible at remembering names," you'll remain terrible at remembering names. If you're convinced you can't do something, you'll never be able to—no matter how simple.

Before you can realize your enormous potential as a public speaker, you must first believe it's possible. So say the following now and often, loudly and with conviction:

I am an excellent public speaker.
I feel fantastic in front of a crowd.
I seek out and look forward to public speaking opportunities.

Don't be shy! This may seem a little silly. But trust me—it will really help. It's OK to whisper or simply mouth the words if you're in public. But really, go ahead and say:

I am an excellent public speaker.

I feel fantastic in front of a crowd.

I seek out and look forward to public speaking opportunities.

It was Henry Ford who said, "Whether you think you can or think you can't—you're right." And it was my mother who always told me, "Never run yourself down—there will always be someone else to do that for you." So whether you're thinking about your speaking abilities in general or a particular presentation, nurture your positive inner voice, and put a muzzle on anything negative.

In fact, when negativity creeps in, simply *let those thoughts go*. Recognize them for what they are—pointless distractions that are completely beneath you. Then just let them pass on through your consciousness without further attention.

Remind yourself of past successes (in any area of your life), visualize future successes, and remind yourself that you're putting in the work to fully realize your potential as an outstanding public speaker. You're not here to simply survive on stage. You're here to *dominate.*

DECIDE TO DOMINATE

I once had a student named Tron Dareing. What an awesome name! I always imagined Tron rock climbing and completing secret agent missions on the weekends, which probably wasn't true...or healthy for the instructor-student relationship. But with a name like *Tron Dareing,* he *had* to be doing super cool stuff, right?

While Tron's presentations were always good, his third of three was simply outstanding. He was comfortable and confident, his silent message, timing and body language were simultaneously natural, inviting and powerful, and he expertly conveyed his ideas with grace and fluidity. Tron was a star that day. His presentation was considerably better than his previous two, and the best the class had seen in some time.

When I went to congratulate him after class, Tron smiled knowingly and said, "Since this was my last presentation, I decided to *dominate* it." Tron was a humble guy, and didn't say this in a cocky way. Rather, he simply exuded the satisfaction of someone who had just accomplished a worthy goal—one that was consciously pursued.

Notice that Tron didn't "hope," "want," or "expect" to do well. Tron *decided* to *dominate.* This is insightful, for one of the most powerful things you can do to realize your potential as a speaker is to resist the temptation to settle for second best, and commit to becoming overwhelmingly successful. This works for most anything, not simply public speaking.

For example, titling this book *Public Speaker as Teacher* might have captured the thesis, and *Your New Public Speaking Coach* might have been more inviting. But committing early to go with *The Best Public Speaking Book* generated a sense of optimism, drive and personal accountability that was absolutely integral to its success.

The same has been true in my personal life. By deciding to be an *outstanding* husband and father, my family is far happier and fulfilled than it would be had I settled for OK. This doesn't mean I'm perfect. I sometimes respond to negativity with negativity, set a bad example for the kids, lose my cool, and do things I regret. But by constantly recommitting to my vision of the encouraging, patient, wise and loving family man I've fully decided to be, the vision slowly becomes reality, one day at a time.

The extra good news is that when you act on your decision to dominate, this not only increases your likelihood of success, but dramatically decreases any associated anxiety. As Dale Carnegie says in *How to Stop Worrying and Start Living,* "I find that fifty percent of my worry vanishes once I arrive at a clear, definite decision; and another forty percent usually vanishes once I start to carry out that decision."

So decide that you don't simply feel good in front of a crowd, but that you feel dominant. Don't simply hope that you'll become an acceptable public speaker, but decide that you're fan-freaking-tastic. Then do something to bring those goals about—they're fully within your grasp. After all, you're taking the time to read and implement The *Best* Public Speaking Book, right?

THE MIND-BODY LOOP

Paul McKenna explains in *I Can Make You Confident* that there's a two-way psycho-physiological connection between posture and mindset. The way we feel impacts our posture, and more importantly, our posture impacts the way we feel. McKenna calls this connection the "mind-body loop."

While it's often difficult to simply *choose* to feel more confident or relaxed, we can indirectly accomplish the same goal by adjusting the way we carry ourselves. For example, think of a time when you felt exceptionally self-confident and relaxed, or imagine a person you consider to be self-confident and relaxed. Now, reflect on your or that person's posture. It most likely includes shoulders back but loose, head up straight, belly in, and chest out. Whatever your current posture, adjust it to adopt those traits.

Notice anything? When we sit, stand and move as a more confident and relaxed version of ourselves would sit, stand and move, we actually begin to become more confident and relaxed. We decide with our minds to adjust our body, and in turn our bodies positively impact our minds. That's the loop!

Of course, the good posture habit is worth doing all the time, not just when giving a presentation. Depending on your current posture habits, it may feel awkward and uncomfortable at first. But stick with it. Your muscles will soon strengthen and your ligaments will adjust, such that the upright, confident you will become the natural you, and you'll enjoy a happier and more positive psyche as a result.

So the next time you're feeling especially anxious or down, it's important to release any negative thoughts and amplify any positive thoughts. But you can also kick-start and speed your recovery by first correcting your posture.

DRESS FOR SUCCESS

In the same way posture can impact your psyche, so too can the clothes you wear. Author Tony Alessandra suggests (and I agree) that it's worth your time and money to invest in a wardrobe that makes you feel good.

What that looks like depends on your personal style, and is likely to change over time. When I was in the military, I felt most comfortable in camouflage. When I was teaching, I felt most comfortable in a button-up shirt and slacks. After a few months in an office setting, I felt most comfortable in a suit and tie.

However, some people absolutely hate ties. If that's you, by all means, don't wear one! And if you're not sure whether a tie is right for you, an important presentation isn't the time to experiment. I suspect the same is true of high heels.

We'll talk more about what Alessandra calls our "silent message" and how we can consciously mold it to suit our public speaking goals in Chapter Four. For now the point is that one way to stave off and decrease nervousness is to dress for success. But whatever you wear, don't wear it because it looks good on someone else. Wear it because it looks good on you, and it's true to who you really are.

BREATHE

One of the first things boxing coaches teach new students is how to breathe. Why would an aspiring fighter need to be reminded of something so simple? Because while hitting others is a huge stress reliever, the idea of getting hit is a huge stress builder. One way our body deals with it is by clamming up and constricting our breath. This may have helped our ancestors hide from predators, but it's apt to make a boxer light-headed, and consequently slower and easier to knock out.

Breathing is equally important for public speakers. You most likely won't be dodging punches, but your brain definitely needs oxygen to remember your talking points and keep you on track. One simple way to calm your nerves as your presentation approaches and to align your thoughts during transitions is to take a slow, deep breath.

Don't attempt to recite your entire presentation on one exhale, and don't breathe so hard that your audience can see or hear it. But do deeply inhale and exhale at a relaxed pace, both before you begin, and occasionally while you're speaking, and your mind will be sharper and your nerves calmer.

BUILD ASSERTIVENESS WITH THE URBAN HONEY BADGER

In civilized society, physical intimidation is rarely overt. However, it's often implicitly conveyed in a person's tone, expressions, and body language. The pushy car salesman may not directly threaten to punch you if you don't accept his terms, but he may subtly convey as much by standing up, putting his hands on his desk and leaning toward you as the sales contract is presented.

Most of us wouldn't be too frazzled by this. We know the salesman isn't going to hit us, even if he wants to give that impression so we'll sign on the dotted line. However, when we're sensitive to this sort of intimidation, we're more easily pushed around. And that general physical insecurity diminishes our general self-confidence and tends to make us more shy and less outspoken.

Sometimes nervousness in public speaking is the result of a physical insecurity of this sort. We're uncomfortable with physical confrontation, and while there's little risk our audience will attack us, we're reluctant to expose ourselves or share our ideas, which generates anxiety.

However, one way to resolve this tension and build confidence is to learn a thing or two about self-defense. That's why I began teaching martial arts in my public speaking classes long ago.

I've used the Urban Honey Badger drill you're about to learn to help hundreds of otherwise timid students overcome long-standing shyness. By learning to confront and ward off an attacker, they became comfortable with the idea of standing up for themselves in other ways as well, and as a result, didn't feel nearly as vulnerable on stage.

The exercise mixes the teachings of three respected self-defense experts: Sigung Richard Clear of Clear's Silat (Silat is an Indonesian martial art known for its fluidity, viciousness, and use of weapons), a former undercover policeman who goes by the name "SouthNarc," and Rich Dimitri, creator of a simple but devastatingly effective close-range technique called the "Shredder." Many thanks to each of these great teachers for all they've contributed to the field of personal defense. All three are worthy of further study.

So here's the drill: Imagine you're on a street corner late at night, in a notoriously dangerous area, when you notice someone walking directly toward you with a scowl and menacing body language.

Once it's obvious they're coming at you and not the vending machine beside you, you need to engage them both physically and verbally as soon as possible to let them know you see them, and that you're not afraid to confront them. If you're not already, turn to face them, bring up one hand into the "halt" position, and ask, "Can I help you with something?" Go ahead—practice right now. Imagine the scenario, and take the initiative to confront this potential attacker with both a question and a hand gesture.

The specific words you use aren't nearly as important as how you say them. You may say, "Can I help you?" but your body, your face, and the inflection in your voice should actually convey, "BOTHER SOMEONE ELSE." Your demeanor shouldn't be overly aggressive—you're not looking for a fight; you're attempting to prevent an assault. However, there should be no tone of timidity or accommodation in your voice. Make it clear that while you're being pleasant for the moment, you are fully prepared to take it to the next level.

If the person never meant you any harm, he'll stop, answer your question, and be on his way. "Yeah, I was just looking for First Street. Know where it is?" But if he continues to approach, you need to elevate your assertiveness by transitioning from a question to a command, and from one physical barrier to two.

Firmly and with moderate volume, say "STOP" as you raise your second hand into the halt position. Whatever level of forcefulness you used in step one, double it in step two. You need to make it painfully clear that you do not appreciate this person's aggression, and that you are not going to passively take whatever it is they're apparently giving. If "HOLD IT RIGHT THERE" feels more natural, that phrase works just as well.

If after asking your opening question, transitioning into a command, and clearly displaying the international sign for halt, this person *still* continues to approach, assume he intends to do you serious harm, and as loudly and as powerfully as you can, yell "GET BACK! GET BACK!" Show them your "war face," crouch down into a fighting stance, and pump both hands aggressively with each syllable. Punctuate your commands with profanity if you're so inclined—this is no time for manners.

If the above sounds like the sort of thing you'd have trouble doing, you're not alone. Step three is where shy students often cower, cover their face, or break into laughter. But they're precisely the students who most need to practice the drill. Assailants feast on complacent and timid victims, and pleading or reasoning with them is unlikely to help, for if assailants were merciful or reasonable, they probably wouldn't be assailants.

I actually used this technique to de-escalate a potential assault in a library parking lot, of all places. My wife and I were loading our kids into our car when I noticed two men approaching from the rear. I overheard a female who was with them anxiously whisper, *"What are you doing?"* and my spider-sense immediately kicked in. I threw up a halt hand and asked, "Can I help you?" in the firm way I described above. The two men began to fan out, continued their approach, and the closest one asked if I had a light. I replied, "No, I do NOT have a light," maintaining the halt hand and general "BOTHER SOMEONE ELSE" body language and tone. After only a few more steps, they slowed their approach, stopped, turned, and walked away.

Whether they really just wanted a light or something else, we'll never know. But whatever the case, the technique kept two potential threats from getting close enough to harm me or my family, and standing up to them in that way felt really good…at least once the adrenaline wore off!

The technique also worked for a former student named Zach, who was walking in front of the campus library when a man stopped him and asked for a light. (I have no idea what's up with chain-smokers at the library!) When Zach kindly told him no, the man pressed forward, exclaiming, "Oh I think you DO have a light—*you DO have a light!*" Zach immediately began pumping both hands and yelling, "GET BACK! GET BACK!" which startled the man, who took a step back in puzzlement, giving Zach the chance he needed to run to safety. Now, maybe the guy just *really* needed a smoke. But more likely he was asking for a light as a ruse to get close enough to do some sort of harm. Luckily Zach didn't give him that chance.

The final portion of the Urban Honey Badger only happens if an assailant makes physical contact, and should only be employed when you're in reasonable fear of serious bodily injury or death. And actually, I'm not going to get that graphic here. Let's just say it involves mauling an assailant's soft targets in ultraviolent fashion—google "Rich Dimitri Shredder" to learn more.

Go ahead—give the Urban Honey Badger drill a try. You've already recited the "*I am an excellent public speaker—*

I feel fantastic in front of a crowd" mantra from above. You might as well do this crazy exercise too!

As you practice, get mean. Get loud. Get aggressive. Decide that you will NOT be a passive victim—in any area of your life—and that those who would take advantage of you will regret any such attempt. Find a place where no one will mind your yelling, and give those imaginary bad guys and earful!

If you're finding it difficult to muster the enthusiasm to practice with conviction, just imagine you're protecting a loved one. I once taught the Urban Honey Badger to a reluctant grandmother who I could barely convince to stand up, let alone shout. But as soon as I threatened her grandbabies, she went crazy! Ms. Iris, I pray no one ever suffers your wrath!

Last, if this drill really resonated with you, sign up for a martial arts class. Experts argue over which style is most effective on the street, but studying any system is better than studying no system. The key is to switch from thinking of yourself as the prey to thinking of yourself as the predator—at least when forced to do so. You're a honey badger, darnit. Cobras don't eat you. *You eat cobras!*

FAKE IT 'TIL YOU MAKE IT

Maybe you're not as assertive as a honey badger just yet. But Aristotle taught that if we seek to possess a trait or virtue, we should act in every instance as if we already possess it. That is, if you want to be more assertive at work, more loving at home, or more disciplined and ambitious in your free time, beyond making the decision to bring the change about, act as if it's already occurred, and soon it shall.

We can of course use this technique to grow as speakers. Simply imagine the sort of speaker you desire to become, and in everything you do, go ahead and *be* that person. In your preparation, your practice and your delivery, act as if your personal speaking vision has become a reality, and it will.

We can also use this technique to promote success for specific presentations, and to even overcome nervousness. The phrase to remember is: *Fake it 'til you make it.*

Although nervousness has a tendency to crescendo as a presentation approaches, it almost always dissipates a couple of minutes in—it's just a matter of getting over that initial hump. The same is often true for athletes. A football player who was a nervous wreck prior to kickoff is instantly calm and focused after his first hit. Players will often speed this transition by slamming into one another pre-game.

As a speaker, I don't advise that you tackle anyone backstage to warm up. But one way to overcome that early nervousness hump more quickly is to concentrate on appearing as if you're confident and in control until your mind matches your body.

This trick works on at least two levels. First, there's McKenna's mind-body loop we just discussed. Confident speakers display confident posture, and when you physically behave as if you're fully comfortable and confident, your mind soon becomes comfortable and confident as well.

Second, there's an external speaker-audience loop. Whether or not you actually feel confident, if you can display the outward appearance of confidence, your audience will respond positively. They'll think, "Wow—anyone *that* sure of themselves *must* have something important to say!" Their good vibes will work their way to the front of the room, and once you soak them in, your fake confidence will transform into genuine confidence.

So remember: as your presentation approaches, regardless of what you're feeling inside, behave as if you're fully calm and in control. When you appear confident and relaxed, not only will this positively influence the mind-body loop, but your audience will look upon you more favorably, which you'll sense, and cause you to feel even better. Before you know it your words will flow naturally, your audience will be attentive, those butterflies will disappear, and bam—you're a successful speaker. So take it from Aristotle. Speed that transition. Fake it 'til you make it.

IF NERVOUSNESS HAPPENS, JUST WORK ON THROUGH

Sometimes despite FM-AC, despite knowing your material, despite developing the right mindset, despite the assertiveness drills, and despite faking it until you make it, nervousness still happens.

A few months ago I got really nervous leading up to and during a particular presentation. My voice wavered, my hands shook, and an irrational fear and panic grew and grew, no matter how hard I tried to reason it away. My nervousness crossed over from mental to physical, much more than it had in years. And to make matters worse, I thought, "I can't get this nervous—I'm writing a book on public speaking!"

Then about a month later I got dry mouth for the first time. In this case as in the last, I perceived the stakes to be relatively high, and my comfort level was relatively low. But this time things were made worse by the fact that I was presenting from a spot where a few years prior, a president had given a speech.

The good news is that in both cases I was able to power through the nervousness without missing a beat. In the first situation, I caught myself worrying that the audience would notice my shaky voice and think less of me for it. But of course, they couldn't. I've had dozens of students apologize for their shaky voice after a presentation, but hardly ever did I notice it. Key lesson: Don't let the fear that others can tell you're nervous amplify your nervousness, because they probably can't.

In the second situation I was more surprised than anything. "Why in the world is my mouth so dry? I bet President Obama's mouth didn't go dry!" Luckily that presentation included a built-in break, so I was able to reset my saliva while the second speaker said a few words. But even without that break, I would have been fine, for I simply slowed down, pronounced my words more methodically, and reminded myself that no one could tell my mouth was dry but me.

So remember that conquering nervousness doesn't always mean preventing it. Sometimes it just can't be avoided. When it happens, the trick is simply powering on through. Breathe, ensure you're holding a confident posture, and mentally regroup; soon that sensation will pass, and you'll do just fine.

ACTION CURES FEAR

Most of what you're learning applies to nervousness that occurs immediately before or during a presentation. However, anxiety can be just as disruptive weeks and even months before a talk. David Schwartz sums up how to overcome this sort of anticipatory anxiety in *The Magic of Thinking Big* with a single phrase: "Action cures fear."

A few years ago I volunteered to play in an alumni basketball game to benefit my old elementary and junior high schools in Vonore, Tennessee. It was supposed to be just for fun, but since I had been an athletic underachiever in school, I let my competitiveness get the better of me, and came to see the game as a chance to prove that I was finally good at sports.

I perceived the stakes to be very high: I could redeem my athleticism or confirm that I *still* wasn't any good at sports. And at first I didn't feel prepared or confident at all. However, rather than dwelling on how I rode the bench and struggled when I was a kid, or worrying that I might repeat that pattern as an adult, I got to work practicing ball handling, passing and shooting. I watched instructional videos, played pick-up games with friends, and drove my poor wife crazy dribbling in the house.

Schwartz was right! The more I practiced, the better I got, and the better I felt about the game. By tip off my anxiety was completely gone, and I was eager to get out there and play. When I scored more points in one evening than I had in all previous games combined, it felt absolutely fantastic. Never mind that it was just for fun!

Practicing cured my anxiety about the alumni game. But what can speakers do to cure long-range public speaking anxiety? First, as soon as you know you'll be giving a presentation, start thinking about the overall goal of your talk. Once that's clear, sketch the main points you'll need to convey, reflect on how to best order them, and draft a few examples you might use to illuminate your ideas.

Second, if you're feeling antsy, pinpoint the problem. Are you worried about a lack of clarity of purpose? About who might be in the audience? About how long you'll be expected to speak? Whether there will be other speakers? Whether you'll have access to a projector? All of the above?

In each of these cases, a quick phone call, email or visit will shed light on the unknown, which will enable you to FM-AC. If the purpose of your presentation is unclear, clarify it. If you're unsure who will be in the audience, ask. If you're concerned about how long you'll be expected to speak, negotiate. If you don't know whether a projector will be available, find out, and bring your own if necessary.

In each case, isolate the issue, clarify the unknowns, and take immediate steps to overcome potential obstacles. You'll feel better as the presentation approaches, and do a better job as a result.

Key Takeaways

➲ Replace worry with **action**

➲ Study and **internalize** your material

➲ Wear clothes that make you feel **good**

➲ Boost your **assertiveness** by practicing the Urban Honey Badger

➲ In all things, **FM-AC**

Chapter Three

DEVELOPING A CLEAR & MEMORABLE PRESENTATION

The key that distinguishes good from great presenters lies in intelligent message development. The seven steps to my method, which I'll explain below, are:

1. Clarify your goals and sketch an outline
2. Embrace your role as expert and teacher
3. Consider your audience
4. Download and unpack your core message
5. Logically arrange your ideas
6. Backfill with analogies and illustrative examples
7. Revise using Zinsser's Four Principles

1 CLARIFY YOUR GOALS & SKETCH AN OUTLINE

Imagine if military commanders gave their soldiers orders to "Do well" rather than "Take that hill by noon tomorrow." Or if business leaders told their personnel to "Work hard" rather than "Increase profits by 15% by the end of the third quarter." In both cases, success is much more likely with goals that are *SMART*—Specific, Measurable, Attainable, Realistic, and Time-bound.

No need to put a deadline on your presentation goals, but you do need to ask yourself: *What's the point of this presentation? What do I aim to achieve? What do I want my audience to understand, learn, remember or do?*

For example, if I were planning a pre-game speech for my tee ball team, I'd need to reflect on our goals for the season:

→ Have fun
→ Make friends
→ Build confidence
→ Learn tee ball basics

Then I'd need to think about what I could do or say during the ninety seconds between warming up and taking the field that would help bring those goals about:

→ Have fun:
Lead a team cheer (Go, Panthers!)

→ Make friends:
Have team exchange high fives

→ Build confidence:
Compliment each player on some area of improvement

→ Learn tee ball basics:
Reinforce one quick tip from practice

For the final draft we can remove the background goals, and no outline is complete without a proper ordering. The team cheer traditionally comes at the very end, and we should probably exchange high fives before the individual encouragement and the tip from practice. Plus, a little more detail would be nice, so I should add a few sub-bullets. How about:

I.   Have team exchange high fives

II. Compliment each player on some area of improvement

   A. Andrew's patience

   B. Lexi's swing

   C. Miles's defense

   D. Amelia's speed

   E. Justin's throwing

   F. Malia's focus

III. Reinforce one quick tip from practice

   A. Remember to twist your whole body when you swing

IV. Lead team cheer (Go, Panthers!)

We'll talk more about logically ordering and fleshing out your ideas in a moment. The point here is that whatever your speaking opportunity, be sure to clarify your goals at the very beginning, and sketch an outline consistent with those goals as soon as you can.

Everything is subject to revision, but you'll get off to a much better start if you understand your destination, and have a rough idea of how to get there. As Stephen Covey says, in all things, when we "begin with the end in mind," our journey is much more enjoyable, and our chances of success much higher.

2 EMBRACE YOUR ROLE AS EXPERT & TEACHER

It doesn't matter if I'm discussing *The Giving Tree* with third graders, teaching awareness and avoidance to self-defense students, or briefing federal leaders on human resource ethics— presentations go better when I think of myself as an expert and teacher.

Thinking of yourself as an expert clarifies the expectation that you'll know what you're talking about. And thinking of yourself as a teacher—whether you'll be presenting in an official classroom setting or not—reinforces the idea that it's your job to effectively convey what you know. The result is that you'll show up much better prepared, much more comfortable than you'd otherwise be, and your audience will learn much more than they otherwise would.

Note the importance of being both expert *and* teacher. We've all known experts in their field who were poor communicators. And at the same time, we've all known charismatic, passionate teachers who simply didn't have much to teach. Our aim is to embody the best of each—to have something to say, as well as the ability and discipline to effectively convey it.

If you happen to be presenting on a topic you know little about, the beauty of public speaking is that studying your subject and organizing your ideas will make you a quasi-expert in the process. The old adage, "If you want to master a subject, teach it" is true for this very reason.

Whether you initially know anything about it or not, you can teach almost anyone almost anything by using a simple three-step process: *relate, unpack, and reinforce.* Whatever your topic, connect it to something your audience already understands, explain how the two are similar, and clarify the nuances.

For example, when my son was three, he asked me to teach him about hockey. So I related it to a game he already understood and enjoyed—soccer. "Hockey is soccer with sticks...on ice." The connection with soccer enabled him to envision goals on either end of an icy playing area, through which players would attempt to knock...*something* with sticks.

I explained that that something was called a "puck"—a smooth rock shaped like a big Oreo cookie—and that the players wore special shoes similar to his roller skates, except with metal blades on the bottom instead of wheels. In just a few seconds he knew a whole lot about hockey, mainly because I had related it to things he already understood: soccer, cookies, and roller skates.

You can teach almost anyone almost anything this same way—by relating new knowledge to existing knowledge. However, different people tend to learn better in different ways. Some learn best by hearing, some by seeing, others by focusing on the big picture, and others by examining the smaller parts. Education experts call these the verbal, visual, global and analytic learning styles.

As a professor, I would sometimes give a survey at the beginning of a new semester designed to assess my students' dominant learning styles. These were more for my students' benefit than mine, for I always had some students who were dominant verbal (learned best via language), some who were dominant visual (needed images), some who were dominant global (preferred big-picture explanations), and some who were dominant analytic (required the small-picture details). Since I was responsible for teaching all of them—not just those who happened to belong to the most common learning style—it was necessary to address every style throughout the semester.

The same is true for you and your audiences. They'll bring a mix of learning styles so you'll need to engage all four, which can sound a little intimidating at first. However, most of us do this automatically. Just imagine any coach giving any halftime locker room speech anywhere around the world. What do you see? Is she simply explaining her strategy for the second half with her voice (verbal)? Or is she drawing X's and O's on a chalkboard (visual)? Is she only talking about high-level strategy (global)? Or is she also giving guidance to individual players (analytic)? Chances are good that she's addressing all four learning styles without even trying.

You won't always have a chalkboard at your disposal. But you will always have your voice, and you can use it to paint images in the minds of your visual learners—just like I painted an image of a locker room scene in your mind with the paragraph above.

So accept and remember that as a public speaker you're an expert and a teacher. Seriously study your subject matter, be able to relate it to something your audience already understands, and keep those four learning styles in mind as you develop your material. But don't sweat over them too much. You're likely to address all four without even trying.

3 CONSIDER YOUR AUDIENCE

People are people. So long as you clearly communicate a logically arranged message with good examples that connect your
new information to information they already understand, any
human should be able to absorb and retain it. However, the
exact language you use, how deeply you delve into your subject, your areas of emphasis and the content of your examples
need to be tailored according to the background and perspective of your audience.

For example, say you're giving a thirty-minute presentation on rocket boosters, and your goal is to give your audience
as comprehensive an understanding of rocketry as you possi-
bly can. If you'll be speaking to kindergarteners, you'll need to
keep things very basic. You might begin with a countdown to
get their attention: "Three, two, one, BLAST OFF!" then
pass around a model rocket or two for the kids to examine.
You'll need to illustrate your key points with examples they
can appreciate, such as, "The body of a rocket is a cylinder,
like Oscar from Sesame Street's trash can." And given their
short attention spans, you might talk for five minutes and
spend the other twenty-five helping them build model rockets
of their own.

On the other hand, if your audience is chemical engineering graduate students, your explanations can be much more
abstract and complex, and your learning goals much more

ambitious. Feel free and encouraged to use complex equations—engineering students love equations! And if your audience is somewhere in-between—perhaps smart laypeople like me—just consider what you can reasonably expect them to know, and adjust accordingly.

It's also smart to consider what your audience desires to get out of your talk. For example, people in leadership positions, such as owners, high-level managers, and executives, are paid to steer organizations from above. As a result, their schedules are typically packed with a constant flow of decision-making responsibilities. That's why leaders prefer and appreciate presentations that are concise, to the point, and pitched in a way that helps them connect the immediate issue with the big picture.

If I were a baseball team manager given thirty minutes to brief the owner on equipment needs, I wouldn't bore her with a long lecture on the history of sports equipment, or opine on the laziness of the bat boys. From the executive's perspective, these issues are either irrelevant or someone else's responsibility.

Instead, I'd present the main context around the key decision. Given that baseball teams are businesses, she'd likely be interested in cost-effectiveness—which specific pieces of equipment, brands and models are best, the reasons for considering them better than the competition, and how much better we could expect the players to perform with them in light of the costs.

I would also be wise to build in a few extra minutes for discussion. People in leadership positions almost always request clarification, so I could plan to use the last ten minutes to answer questions with honesty and to the best of my ability, and promise to get back to her on anything I couldn't answer on the spot. It would also be a good idea to close on schedule, for while speakers should always be respectful of their audience's time, it's smart to be extra mindful of the clock the further you go up any chain of command.

In most cases your audience will be a very diverse group, and you will only be able to make very rough generalizations about them. However, do give them some consideration when developing your message, and tailor your approach to their likely backgrounds, interests and expectations. Kindergarteners like Sesame Street, grad students like equations, and leaders like concision.

4 DOWNLOAD & UNPACK YOUR CORE MESSAGE

At this point you've clarified your goals, fully embraced your role as expert and teacher, considered your audience, and are ready to add some serious meat to the presentation skeleton you sketched in step one. And while you may be tempted to take what you have to the stage, my advice is that you further refine and develop it behind the scenes.

Any quality presentation I've ever given required reflection, reorganization and revision, either on paper or the computer screen. I've thrown together shoddy presentations on the spur of the moment that got the job done. But every one of them would have been much, much better if I'd taken the time to thoroughly unpack, revise and organize my ideas.

This is because understanding is increased dramatically when we download our ideas into some external medium where they can be better developed, examined, arranged, polished, and finally reabsorbed for transfer to others. Think of this like math. We can work through simple equations in our head without much trouble. But add too many variables and too many steps and it's too hard to track all the moving parts. However, that same complex problem is fully manageable when we write it down and work through it on paper. The same is true for developing and arranging a presentation.

For example, say I've been asked to brief a fresh crop of congressional interns on Metro (subway) escalator etiquette in Washington DC. Maybe a really smart person could work up a fantastic presentation on the fly. But I'd begin by downloading my initial thoughts in bullet point form, like this:

→ If you stand on the left side, you're going to irritate the locals

→ The left side is like the fast lane

→ Tourists often make this mistake

→ When I first got to DC I thought this was crazy, but within a week I was walking on the escalator too

Once I've downloaded my thoughts, the next step is to identify the key theme that captures the whole. Regardless of how complex it may initially seem, every topic can be boiled down into a sentence. For example, "Good parenting requires love, patience, and a willingness to overlook your kid's mistakes, and forgive your own." Or, "Though Marx's account of the problems of capitalism is somewhat insightful, his solutions are neither morally required nor practically feasible." Or, "Public speaking requires only two core traits: the courage to get up there and the determination to get better." As a speaker, it's your job to figure out that one-sentence summary.

A draft core message for the Metro escalator etiquette presentation might be: *If you're going to stand on the escalator, please scoot over to the right.* However, points that I failed to include in my original list that are worth considering include both the why behind the custom, and the qualifier not to take it personally if you get yelled at.

The Why: It's important to leave the left side of the escalator open for walking because a) many Metro riders have (what they consider) important meetings to attend, and getting there on time sometimes requires extreme measures, and b) many people use Metro to connect with Amtrak, MARC (Maryland's commuter rail system) and VRE (Virginia's commuter rail system)—each of which run on a very tight schedule. Missing your connection can mean the difference between arriving five minutes early and eight hours late.

You're Excused: For the most part, people who work and live in DC realize that walking on the escalator is odd and are therefore understanding when visitors inadvertently back up the flow. So don't take it personally if people yell in your general direction, asking folks to please walk on the left. They're not taking it personally either.

Given that this is a pretty simple topic, and my main points are on the page, there's not much else to do. But before I finalize and print an outline, I need to ensure everything flows in a logical order. A confusing order leads to a confusing presentation, which leads to a confused audience.

5 LOGICALLY ARRANGE YOUR IDEAS

When it comes to organizing your message, that old cliché— *Tell them what you're going to tell them, tell them, and then tell them what you've told them*—is so often repeated because it works. Audiences better understand and remember ideas that are introduced early, clearly explained and reinforced. Therefore, the basic structure that works for most any presentation is introduction, preview, body, recap and close. Depending on your subject, audience and occasion, you might add elaborations and clarifications, perhaps like this:

I. **Introduction**: Hi, I'm Matt—thanks so much for coming out

II. **Preview**: Today I'm going to teach you a bit about x, y and z

III. **Body**: x, y and z (include examples)

IV. **Elaborations**: Extra stuff about x, y and z

V. **Clarifications**: You may think x and y are the same, but they're not—here's why

VI. **Recap**: High points about x, y and z

VII. **Close**: Thank you so much for your attention!

For the escalator etiquette presentation, we might arrange the ideas like this:

I.   **Introduction:** Hi, I'm Matt—thanks so much for coming out.

II.   **Preview:** Today I'm going to teach you a bit about Metro escalator etiquette in Washington DC.

III.   **Body:** Walk on the left and stand on the right. Whether you're transferring from the Metro to Amtrak at Union Station, or from the Red line to the Orange line at Metro Center—in all cases, walk on the left and stand on the right.

IV.   **Elaborations:** Just like on the highway, the right lane is for slower traffic, and the left lane is for passing.

V.   **Clarifications:** This isn't expected in really touristy spots, like inside the Smithsonian Air and Space Museum, and if you forget and people call you out, don't sweat it—they're just in a hurry, and probably forgive you.

VI.   **Recap:** Remember to walk on the left and stand on the right.

VII. **Close:** Thank you so much for your attention!

For me, the intro and close are almost always the same. I begin by introducing myself and thanking the audience for coming, and close by thanking them for their attention. The middle is pretty standard as well—I get the main idea on the table, explain it in a couple of different ways, elaborate, clarify, and reiterate. This template works in most contexts, but not always.

For example, playing host at a comedy club is a special public speaking opportunity with several unique duties, and many transitions. When I used to do it on weekends, my routine would look like this: I'd first welcome the audience, preview the evening's comics, announce upcoming shows, plug the club's promo items, deliver my five-minute joke set (my highlight of the evening), introduce the feature act, thank the feature act and introduce the headliner, thank the headliner, and close the show with a drawing, a song, and an invitation to meet the comics in the lounge. Whew!

If I'd followed my standard model and previewed my jokes in the beginning—"Tonight I'll tell two jokes about parenting and three about teaching"—and recapped the high points at the end—"Don't forget that the punchline to my first joke was 'Unless you're Godzilla!' and the punchline to my last joke was 'Burn her house down!'"—they wouldn't have been nearly as funny.

So you're of course free and encouraged to arrange your material whichever way works best, which depends on your style, message, and circumstances. The shorter and the more basic the presentation, the more steps you can skip. But whether you adopt this template or customize your own, you'll need to consider how to order the content in your body. There are several ways to do this, each better suited to different types of information.

If you'll be delivering an argumentative or persuasive presentation, you might explain your issue, preview your current view, logically support it with reasons, and preemptively respond to potential objections. If your material involves a historical account of a series of events, or future steps to be taken in a particular order, presenting your points chronologically will make them easier to follow and understand.

For example, in a recent presentation on the historical expansion of high school ethics bowls, I projected a plain map of the US with the heading "Beginning of Time–2003." (Ethics bowls are similar to traditional debates, except participants are not required to disagree, and are not assigned positions, but are invited to think through difficult moral and political issues according to their own lights, using disinterested reason as their guide. The team with the most compelling argument wins!) When I clicked to the next slide, the heading changed to "2004," Utah turned green, and I explained how Professor

Karen Mizell at Utah Valley University organized the very first high school bowl that year, based on the successful Intercollegiate Ethics Bowl. Each time I changed slides the date would change and different states would turn green—New Jersey, then North Carolina, Tennessee, New York, Florida, California, Maryland, Pennsylvania, Massachusetts, and DC. I went all the way up to the present day, explaining details about the different bowl organizers across the US, and even made some projections about bowl growth in the next ten years—providing commentary on how I envisioned this changing America's political culture for the better. In this case, since the topic concerned a historical progression, a chronological ordering worked best.

If your topic concerns sub-parts that somehow work together, you can explain the whole then break down each part, or explain the parts and work up to the whole. Or you can even jump into the middle and work your way out, which is exactly what I'd do if explaining how the body's organs and organ systems work together to sustain life.

I'd begin by covering how the nervous system controls our muscles, how the digestive system enriches our blood with nutrients, and how the circulatory system delivers those nutrients for the other systems to use. However, a presenter could just as well begin with the heart and work her way up, or begin with the entire body and work her way down.

You can also organize your topic according to conceptual complexity, or according to the importance of the ideas, or according to an order dictated by someone else. Just arrange your content in whichever way will best facilitate communication. And when it appears that several different approaches would likely work equally well, go with whichever best resonates with your personality or seems easiest.

Last, though it can take some work, logically ordering your presentation has the added benefit of making it easier for you to remember your talking points. When your ideas naturally flow from one to the next, you won't have to put much effort into memorization beyond your opening section. Once you get started, everything will automatically fall into place.

For example, the first day in my ethics classes would go something like this: After a warm welcome and mutual introductions, I'd explain that philosophy is the reason-based attempt to answer life's big non-empirical questions, which would naturally lead to the differences between empirical and non-empirical questions, which would naturally lead to the nature of ethical questions, which would naturally lead to an exploration and eventual refutation of moral relativism, which would naturally lead to the alternative of moral objectivism, which would naturally lead to the four dominant ethical theories, which we would naturally apply to particular ethical issues.

You may not be versed in philosophy, but you don't need to be to appreciate the point. Once we got rolling, there wasn't anything for me to remember. Presenting was simply a matter of following where reason led. And in terms of retention, if a student could remember any one part of the class, he or she could recall what came both before and after it by asking why we were discussing that topic, and what we would have likely discussed next.

For all of these reasons, take the time to logically arrange your presentations. Whether you're rallying a tee ball team, briefing congressional interns, exploring the complexities of philosophical ethics, or something else, it'll make your presentation easier for your audience to understand, and easier for everyone to remember—including you.

6 Backfill with Analogies & Illustrative Examples

Once your main ideas are clearly articulated and intelligently arranged, it's time to add additional content to help them stick. Analogies are especially useful for this purpose. My son better understood hockey when I related it to soccer, and you better understood DC escalator etiquette when I related it to highway traffic norms.

When creating your own analogies, remember that they don't have to be fancy or complex. In fact, basic, straightforward comparisons are often best. For example, if asked to brief your office on a new computer security policy, rather than belaboring every detail, you could simply explain that it's like the old policy, except the new policy requires users to insert their ID card into a special slot. Or if coaching a group of new mommies and daddies on good parenting, you could tell them that three-year-olds are just like newborns, except three-year-olds eat more and make a bigger mess. In both cases, simple, concise and direct comparisons are very effective.

However, creativity isn't a bad thing. One of my favorite analogies uses the image of an elephant rider to teach the basics of motivational psychology. It was created by University of Virginia psychologist, Jonathan Haidt, and made famous by brothers Chip and Dan Heath in *Switch: How to Change When Change Is Hard.*

The rider, corresponding to our rational side, is good at analyzing, setting goals and planning, but he often lacks the power to actually accomplish those goals. The elephant, corresponding to our emotional side, seeks instant gratification, and while very powerful, is short-sighted and risk averse. Without the rider's guidance, he runs recklessly toward reward and away from perceived danger.

Separately the elephant and rider accomplish little. But together they accomplish much; especially when they have a neatly-cut path to guide their way, which of course corresponds to the desired change.

Less creative authors might have simply said that change managers should engage their audience's hearts and minds with clear step-by-step guidance. Or they might have alluded to Freud's Id and Super Ego. But the rider, the elephant and the path make the interconnecting concepts much more vivid, clear, and likely to stick.

Also, notice how learning about the elephant rider helped you better understand and appreciate the usefulness of analogies. I could have said, "Use analogies—they're awesome," and left it at that. But by reminding you of the hockey and escalator etiquette analogies we'd already covered, and unpacking the elephant and rider analogy, the point was made much more vivid, and your understanding and appreciation are all that much stronger.

This speaks to the fact that ideas are better understood and remembered when illustrated with examples. Here are some examples of examples: When teaching police cadets how to use objects to shield themselves from gunfire, instructors will often demonstrate with both the good example of a brick wall, and the bad example of a cardboard box. And when teaching students how to revise their sentences for clarity and concision, a fan of writing coach William Zinsser might cite both his good example of "Good writing is rewriting," and the made-up bad example of "When an authoring agent undertakes to commit thoughts to paper, he or she accomplishes greater success when writing the second time through in contrast with their first attempt at a written accomplishment." (More on Zinsser's excellent advice in a sec.)

One last thing you can do to reinforce your key points is to use callbacks. A callback is the technique of mentioning something later in a presentation that was mentioned earlier in a presentation. Comedians, politicians, songwriters, screenwriters, and authors use callbacks all the time.

Callbacks are effective communication tools because they reactivate recently activated areas of the brain, which releases serotonin—a substance that we experience as pleasurable. Oh, I don't know if that's true...but it sure sounds good!

Whatever the neurological basis, being made consciously aware of learning is simply enjoyable. When a speaker alludes to something she recently said, it illuminates new conceptual connections. And unless the topic is unpleasant, that's fun—it makes the audience think, "Hey, I remember that!"

Callbacks also help build a relationship. I was honored to host my fourteen-year high school reunion, and since I'd known everyone in the room for at least two decades, I could reference shared experiences that reinforced the group's intimacy—Ms. Lowe's obsession with owls, Coach Webb's constant need for eye drops, and how everyone once thought Lillie was a witch.

However, as speakers, we usually won't know our audiences well enough to talk about the good old days. But we will know them well enough to talk about points we've made earlier in our talk. Highlighting that shared experience—even if it's a very brief and superficial shared experience—will produce feelings of trust and warmth typically reserved for people we know well, and our audiences will look upon us more favorably and be more receptive as a result.

Last, callbacks improve your audience's receptivity by bringing to light their learning. Remembering what you said earlier confirms that they're retaining your message, which is a boost to their view of you as a communicator, and their view of themselves as a learner. For example, in Chapter One I explained that becoming an effective public speaker really only takes two things: the courage to do it and the determination to get better. And as you may have noticed, I've reiterated that key point at least once since, and as you'll soon discover, I'll reiterate it again before we're through. Hopefully this is helping you appreciate and remember the point, illuminating the fact that you're learning, and making you an even more receptive learner as a result.

In summary, analogies, simple comparisons, illustrative examples and callbacks are excellent tools to help you communicate your ideas. But if you only remember one thing from this section, make sure it's to link the ideas you're attempting to communicate to ideas your audience already understands. Doing so will make both teaching and learning much easier and enjoyable.

7 REVISE USING WILLIAM ZINSSER'S FOUR PRINCIPLES

In William Zinsser's now classic book, *On Writing Well*, you'll find four indispensable principles of effective communication. I keep them in mind anytime I'm writing or presenting, as well as anytime I'm teaching others to write or present. I'll briefly share them here, and unpack them below.

Clarity: As Zinsser says, "If it isn't clear, you might as well not write it—you might as well stay in bed." Make certain your words convey exactly what you intend them to convey—no more, no less. The only time it's acceptable for an audience member to wonder what it is you're trying to say is when you're giving a presentation on confusion, and you're in the middle of an illustrative example.

Simplicity: Unnecessarily complex words and phrases block communication and put a barrier between you and your audience. Use simple, straightforward language, and refuse to indulge in pomposity. In fact, "refuse to indulge in pomposity" is a pompous phrase! How about "No fancy talk." No need to pretend to be smarter than you are with an inflated vocabulary. All it's likely to achieve is a confused and alienated audience, which is the opposite of what you want.

Brevity: The human mind can only absorb so much at once, so make your ideas sharp and to the point. Remember: concision is a virtue.

Humanity: Find, embrace and develop your unique voice. As I've always taught my philosophy students, "Don't adopt the style of the authors we'll be reading. Even though they've authored some of the most amazing ideas in human history, communicating them isn't always their strong suit." I liked this principle so much, I made it a pillar of my method. Zinsser and Deaton agree: Be Thyself!

Zinsser's advice is pure gold. If you burden your audience with a muddled message that's unnecessarily complex, they'll tune out, whether they want to learn what you have to say or not. But give them a clear, simple, brief message—and deliver it using your sincere, genuine voice—and they won't be able to help but learn.

However, ideas rarely come out clear, simple, brief and in our own voice the first time. This is why Zinsser teaches that good writing is *re*writing, and why revising your speaking notes and rehearsing your presentations is especially important. Each time through you'll think of new ways to improve—a more logical ordering here, a clearer example there. And while revision and practice take effort, if you expect your audience to give you their time and attention, respect them enough to deliver a polished product.

Creating that polished product is easier when you follow the advice of productivity guru Steve Robbins, author of *The Get-It-Done Guy's 9 Steps to Work Less and Do More*. As Stever explains, scientists recently confirmed what common sense already suggests—that multitasking, while fun, isn't very efficient, and tends to degrade quality. Although switching back and forth among lots of unrelated tasks can be entertaining, it keeps our brains in first gear. But when we focus on similar tasks, our minds acclimate, get in a groove and produce much better results.

Stever recommends that we categorize the items on our to-do lists according to the sort of activities they entail, and tackle one group at a time. When it comes to public speaking, message creation and editing involve different parts of the brain. Therefore, when you're drafting that initial outline or backfilling with analogies, let the ideas flow. Don't stop to judge or analyze them—just get them out of your head and onto the page. Once you're through creating, *then* go back and change, rearrange and polish.

You can't expect your mind to create high-quality content when it's in edit mode, or do high-quality editing when it's in create mode. So when you inevitably see an opportunity to do one activity while you're engaged in another, just insert a note and return to it later. Typing those notes in all caps will help you find them. For example, notes like DEVELOP STEVER TASK SEGREGATION ADVICE HERE and CUT THE CLUTTER IN THIS SECTION were strewn throughout draft versions of this book.

"Cut the clutter" is actually a bonus tip from Mr. Zinsser. Clutter refers to words and phrases that don't contribute new or essential meaning to the ideas you're attempting to convey. Clutter gets in the way of your core message, and has a tendency to distract and confuse your audience. Consider the following sentences:

1. I believe that cutting clutter is the absolute most important activity in which a person can engage when preparing a presentation outline.

> **2.** When preparing your outline, it's very important to cut the clutter.

Though both say essentially the same thing, the first is twenty-two words long, while the second is only eleven. What's the difference? For starters, the phrase "I believe" is unnecessary, for of course I believe what I'm saying. Further, "Activity in which a person can engage" is ridiculously cumbersome. Even the word "presentation" is clutter, for it's obvious from context that the only outline I'd be discussing is a presentation outline.

The second sentence, which lacks all of those flaws, is clearly superior. But it doesn't quite emphasize that cutting the clutter is *the* most important step in outline prep, not simply *an* important step. If that were something I intended to convey, an alternative, coming in at just ten words, might read, "When preparing your outline, clutter cutting is of utmost importance." Simple, clear: clutter-free.

American author and Wall Street Journal columnist Peggy Noonan expertly illustrates clutter cutting with this wonderful example:

Remember the waterfront shack with the sign FRESH FISH SOLD HERE. Of course it's fresh, we're on the ocean. Of course it's for sale, we're not giving it away. Of course it's here, otherwise the sign would be someplace else. The final sign: FISH.

Maybe I could have cut this entire section by just providing that one quote!

Revising your work using Zinsser's principles can be painful. On close inspection, you'll realize that sections you've spent hours developing are irrelevant, unclear, too long-winded, not true to your voice, or simply clutter. And you'll be tempted to leave them in rather than throw away all that hard work. Be strong! Keep and mold ideas directly linked to your presentation goals, and save everything else in a second file entitled "SCRAPS." The SCRAPS file will make clutter psychologically easier to cut, and you'll have it should you change your mind or develop a similar presentation down the road.

Key Takeaways

➲ **Clarify your goals and sketch an outline:** Begin with the end in mind—what you aim to achieve and your essential core message. Doing this sooner rather than later will ease your mind and optimize your preparation.

⊃ **Embrace your role as expert and teacher:** You're expected to understand your subject and be able to transfer that understanding to your audience. Internalize that responsibility now.

⊃ **Consider your audience:** How can you tailor your message to match your audience's background, expectations, and goals? Are they kindergarteners? Grad students? Something in-between?

⊃ **Download and unpack your core message:** Revisit and more fully unpack the skeleton you drafted in step one. For best results, get it out of your head and onto a page or screen.

⊃ **Logically arrange your ideas:** Arrange your material chronologically, according to conceptual complexity, methodologically—whichever order will best facilitate communication and understanding.

⊃ **Backfill with analogies and illustrative examples:** Relate the ideas you intend to communicate to ideas your audience likely already understands. Then clarify the nuances.

⊃ **Revise using Zinsser's four principles:** Revise everything for optimal levels of clarity, simplicity, brevity and humanity. Remember that good writing is rewriting, and be sure to cut all inessential clutter.

Chapter Four

PHYSICAL
DELIVERY

Few scientific "facts" are repeated more often than the adage that seventy percent of communication is non-verbal. I've always considered that estimate high, but if physical delivery is responsible for even five percent of communication, it's definitely worthy of our attention.

Consciously or not, people draw conclusions about our priorities, lifestyle, goals, and even our intelligence and self-worth according to our dress, accessories, posture and mannerisms. Admitting as much doesn't mean this is the way things *should* be. Were humans fully enlightened, we'd judge people for who they really are, if we judged them at all.

The good news is that the silent message we send with our bodies is within our sphere of influence. Rather than ignore, lament or rebel against the fact that we're judged according to our appearance, why not learn to master it instead? All you need to do is wear clothes that make you feel good, stand up straight, move naturally, and use barriers like lecterns only when you actually intend to convey heightened formality or separateness between you and your audience.

If you play the physical delivery game well, you can win your audience's respect and attention long before you even open your mouth. The first and one of the most important steps happens before you even leave home, in the selection of your attire.

Your Silent Message

I was first exposed to the term "silent message" in Tony Alessandra's leadership and relationship development book, *Charisma: Seven Keys to Developing the Magnetism that Leads to Success*. Alessandra does a wonderful job explaining the importance of sincerely listening to others, of having a clear vision, and of working with a team to achieve great things. But most important for our purposes are his insights on the power of the clothes we wear.

In an official speaking setting, jeans usually denote casualness, a tie usually denotes formality, and a visible tattoo usually denotes rebelliousness. All three together denote confusion!

You might think it's always better to err on the conservative side. But what's best for a particular speaking opportunity actually depends on the audience, the venue, and your personal style and communication goals.

For example, imagine if Farmer Brown showed up at the county fair to deliver his presentation on cow-milking in a three-piece suit. In that context, wearing anything fancier than overalls sends the message that he just doesn't have a clue—either about how messy hand-milking a cow can be or about the farming culture.

Academic philosophers have a similar bias against fancy clothes. While sport coats are acceptable, philosophy professors assume anyone who wears a suit must have something to prove, and probably shouldn't be trusted. However, business school professors probably view anyone *not* wearing a suit to be the clueless rookie…or perhaps a socialist spy.

The key is to wear clothes that are true to your personal style, but at the same time promote your particular goals in the context of your audience's biases. Here's what I wrote about my own silent message when I was a graduate teaching associate. It's from an article on public speaking I wrote for my students:

I made a very conscious decision to stop wearing ties several semesters ago. Why? Because I was coming off as more stuffy and formal than I actually am. *My students told me so.* So I dropped that classic symbol of stiffness. I'm still rocking the slacks and dress shirts—just no ties. And that man purse I carry? A conscious decision as well. That's what separates students from teachers, didn't you know? Ever see a professor lugging around a backpack?

When I first started teaching, having been an undergraduate just a few months prior, I wanted to distinguish myself from the rest of the student body. If I had worn a t-shirt and flip flops to class, they might have thought I was cool. But given my role, responsibilities and goals as a professor-in-training, it made sense to present myself as more of an authority than a peer. So out went the backpack, and in came the man purse. Out went the polos, and in came the dress shirts.

Finding the level of formality that best suited my aims and personality took time, and in fact continues to change. The same is true for you, so don't be afraid to update your style as you grow as a speaker, a person, and a professional.

Last, as we previewed in Chapter Two, posture also has a huge impact on your silent message. A well-held spine conveys health, vigor and strength. Slouching conveys a lack of confidence, exhaustion or laziness, and in some cases an acceptance of defeat. Have you ever heard political commentators say, "The president's posture was very aggressive in the last debate"? Or a sports analyst say, "That quarterback has to improve his posture if he's to lead the team to victory"? The posture of the body under the clothes is just as important as the clothes themselves.

Whatever silent message you choose to present, remember that it should align with your immediate and long-term goals, and be true to your personal style. Playing this game is superficial and even a little silly. But so long as humans are going to judge one another according to their posture and attire, we might as well play the game well.

KNOW WHEN TO LECTERN

"You should only deliver your presentation from behind a lectern when the microphone is bolted to it, and you can't find a wrench."

I'm kidding now, but I used to actually teach this. My thinking was that the lectern served as an unnecessary physical barrier, which tended to serve as an unnecessary psychological barrier, which only undermined communication. I'd allow students to use one for their first presentation if they preferred, but by their second I expected them to walk away from it often; by their third I expected it to be used as nothing more than a base for their notes and water.

Dr. Carol Kinsey Goman confirms my early bias in *The Silent Language of Leaders: How Body Language Can Help—or Hurt—How You Lead.* In a section on announcing change, Dr. Goman argues that "a lectern not only covers up the majority of your body but also acts as a barrier between you and your audience," which is typically a bad thing when your aim is to reassure and inspire.

However, while lecterns do imply a degree of separation between speaker and audience, I now think that's not always a bad thing. A senator addressing her colleagues, a CEO addressing her workforce, or even a principal addressing her school might all benefit from sending the implicit message, "I'm the boss here," or, "This is serious stuff."

On the other hand, that same senator, CEO or principal would benefit by going lectern-less under different circumstances. Moving out from behind it conveys comfort and familiarity with your audience. It conveys warmth and an eagerness to collaborate. It also implies that you possess the sort of self-confidence that doesn't require a shield.

I can recall one briefing in particular where a leader had just resigned, and his superior was brought in to reassure everyone that their programs and positions were secure. The speaker might have better conveyed warmth and compassion had he walked amongst the crowd as he spoke. But given that a disruptive change in leadership was underway, conveying strength and stability was more important, and his use of the full-bodied lectern helped communicate exactly that.

In that same assembly room only a few weeks later, the same audience reconvened to discuss a physical merging of employees at remote offices with those at headquarters. This time a different speaker hardly used the lectern at all. Whether it was the result of her naturally warm personality or a conscious decision, she made it clear with both her words and her body language that she understood the audience's concerns about overcrowding and privacy, and would do everything within her power to make the move as smooth as possible. Taking questions, inviting the crowd to brainstorm for solutions, and giving every comment serious consideration added to her effectiveness in this regard. But her positioning amongst the audience most contributed to her implicit message of understanding and solidarity.

In the end, whether and when you should walk among the crowd or remain stationary behind a lectern depends on your style, audience and goals. Like much else in public speaking, the point is to understand the message that each option sends, and pick the correct one in light of your goals.

EYE CONTACT

Eye contact conveys confidence, courage and warmth. It shows that you believe what you're saying and that you're interested in whether your audience accepts and understands it. A lack of eye contact is often perceived as an indication that the speaker has something to hide, or is being deceptive.

So unless they're just too far away to see, or you're blinded by stage lights, make a point to look everyone in your audience in the eye at least once. The only exception is if an audience member has a face tattoo. In that case, *no eye contact—NO EYE CONTACT!*

This, of course, means you shouldn't bring a verbatim speech to the stage to read word-for-word. Unless you're using a teleprompter, it's impossible for your eyes to be on a script and your audience at the same time. Instead, prepare well enough to be able to speak extemporaneously from an outline. Looking down from time to time to ensure you're on track is perfectly fine, so long as you spend the vast majority of your presentation looking at your audience, not your notes. (More on using a script in Chapter Six.)

Also, be sure to spread your attention across your entire audience. Maybe your grandmother is sitting in the front row. But while it's appropriate for Grandma to receive the lion's share of your attention, show the rest of the attendees proper respect by focusing on them as well. Not only will the crowd appreciate it, having a speaker stare at you throughout their entire presentation is just creepy—even for Grandma!

Last, if doing so makes you more comfortable, it's OK to look beyond your audience to imaginary people at the back of the room. You might think of a supportive friend (or even me!) smiling approvingly and encouragingly for an extra boost. (*You're doing great!*) The key is to keep your head up, address the entire audience, and look everyone in the eye at least once. Or, at least, everyone without a face tattoo.

USING VISUAL AIDS

I recently had the pleasure to attend a leadership seminar put on by English author Paul McGee. Paul wrote the bestselling *S.U.M.O. (Shut Up, Move On): The Straight-Talking Guide to Creating and Enjoying a Brilliant Life.* But long before he was an author, Paul was a presenter.

Apart from being a superb communicator, Paul was a master of engaging his audience. He had us paired off doing exercises within the first two minutes, answering insightful questions in our workbooks before first break, laughing and thinking the whole way through. His engagement techniques are more relevant to Chapter Seven. But I mention Paul here because of his expert use of visual aids.

Good visual aids artfully add to the show and help a speaker communicate the key points he or she is attempting to convey. For example, Paul taught us four types of faulty thinking: Inner Critic, Broken Record, Martyr Syndrome, and Trivial Pursuits. I'll let you read the book to learn about the other three, but Inner Critic is that negative voice I mentioned in Chapter Two. It's a useless, destructive voice that for some reason tries to drag us down and beat us up. Rather than just describing it, Paul pulled out a big red boxing glove, which he used to gently punch himself as he spoke. Brilliant! An extremely memorable, spot-on representation of the idea he was attempting to convey—that boxing glove brought the Inner Critic to life in a way mere words never could.

Another visual aid Paul used throughout the seminar was a rubber band. Anytime he talked about how leaders are stretched with competing obligations or pulled in different directions, out came the rubber band. He'd pull it tight, then stretch it a bit more, then a bit more, then a bit more— demonstrating exactly the feeling everyone in the room had experienced at one time or another, and making perfectly clear the importance of taking time to relax.

Last was an aid Paul used in the very beginning, and continually referenced throughout. It was a simple presentation slide displaying a weekly calendar, beginning with Monday and ending with Sunday. What made the slide impactful was the decade of our life displayed beneath each day of the week: 0-10 beneath Monday, 11-20 beneath Tuesday, 21-30 beneath Wednesday, 31-40 beneath Thursday, 41-50 beneath Friday, 51-60 beneath Saturday, and 61-70 beneath Sunday. Some of us are lucky enough to get holidays—a bonus decade or two under an additional Monday or Tuesday.

I don't know about you, but I fully intend to enjoy an extra Wednesday! But the slide still generated the seriousness and sense of urgency Paul was after. He wanted us to feel the need to act on our goals sooner rather than later, and he definitely achieved that aim. For somehow recognizing that I'm on the "Thursday of my life" made my mortality much more vivid and my time much more precious than merely reflecting on a number. Thanks for the extra motivation, Paul!

Think of creative ways to incorporate visual aids into your own presentations. Use them intelligently, deliberately and sparingly. Remember that they should be aids, not distractions—they should add to and amplify the key points you're already making. Everything feeds back into that primary function of public speaking—it's just a particular form of communication, remember?

Key Takeaways

➲ Improving your **posture** will not only improve your confidence—it will give your audience additional reason to pay attention and respect you

➲ Wear clothes that are consistent with your **personality** and promote your goals

➲ Use a lectern when you want to convey **formality**, authority, or separateness

➲ Forego the lectern and walk around when you want to convey **warmth**, empathy, solidarity, or an eagerness to collaborate

➲ Use visual aids to hammer home your **key** ideas

Chapter Five

ORAL DELIVERY

Oral delivery has four main components: *accent, enunciation, volume* and *pace.* Accent concerns the *flavor* of your voice, which should be true to who you are. Enunciation concerns how clearly you pronounce your words. Projection concerns whether or not, and how well, your audience can hear you. Pace concerns how fast or slow your words come out, when and how often that speed is varied, and your tactical use of silence.

However, don't be intimidated by those categories—oral delivery is actually very simple. So long as your audience can hear and understand you, you're good. As always, you're simply aiming to communicate, so don't get caught up in the science of voice resonance or refraction angles. Just speak up, be yourself, and focus on clear communication.

ACCENT

Part of what made JFK such a memorable, effective speaker was his sharp New England accent. His words continue to powerfully impact those who hear them, not *in spite* of his accent, but in part *because* of his accent. Similarly, can you imagine, "I'll be back" or "California" without Arnold

Schwarzenegger's distinct Austrian accent? His voice is an essential part of his multi-million dollar persona, and I doubt he would have achieved the same level of success without it.

I happen to have been blessed with a mild Southern drawl. It's been tempered by time in the military, academia, and DC, but it most definitely remains. It's most noticeable when I pronounce any word with the sound *eye*, such as in *hi, bye,* or *pumpkin pie.* So imagine how Southern I sound at Thanksgiving dinner!

My accent occasionally draws notice. But given that I speak clearly and professionally, and the fact that it's a part of who I am, I haven't tried to change it, and have no plans to do so.

I have the same advice for you. If you're blessed with a Southern, Northern, East Coast, West Coast, Tex-Mex, Pacific Northwest, Canadian, British, Spanish, German, urban, rural or any other accent—go with it. So long as people can understand what you're saying, don't feel any pressure to change the way you talk, either as a public speaker or in private conversation.

Your unique accent is just one component of your authentic stage self, which we'll talk more about in Chapter Eleven: Be Thyself. But as I'll more fully explain when we get there, being true to who you are is completely consistent with improving. So as you develop your public speaking voice, reflect on how you sound when you're confident and in control, as well as how you sound when imagining your ideal public speaking self. Strive to bring *that* voice to the stage—accent and all. It worked for JFK and Arnold, and it can work for you.

ENUNCIATION

If you enunciate well already, feel free to skip this section. But if you're a natural mumbler like me, building your vocal precision is well worth the trouble.

Luckily there's a plethora of free enunciation drills available online. A quick google search will turn up at least a dozen, each set containing a creative phrase for every letter in the alphabet. Bookmark or print your favorites and practice as time allows—while getting ready in the morning, commuting, or right before bed. Pick no more than two or three to practice per session so you can focus on each unique sound.

Pronounce the phrases slowly, overemphasizing each syllable, and consciously noticing how your face, mouth and vocal cords work together. The idea isn't that you should speak like this while giving a presentation, but that methodical practice will improve the clarity of your natural speech, much like methodically practicing a karate kick will improve its accuracy and power in a fight.

Another great way to improve your enunciation is to listen to and repeat vocabulary-building audiobooks. Much like strenuous exercise makes our bodies stronger, and strenuous thought makes our minds stronger, pronouncing unfamiliar consonant and verb combinations makes our enunciation stronger. While you may never use "soliloquy" in a real sentence, carefully reciting it and its definition will help you more clearly enunciate the words you do use. The Princeton Review's *Word Smart: Building a More Educated Vocabulary* audio CDs are great, but excellent free options are out there—just google "vocabulary audiobook" and see what you can find.

Finally, one easy way to improve your enunciation is simply by reading aloud. If you're a parent, kill several birds with one stone by reading to your kids. Few activities are more rewarding for both parties, especially if you pause to engage in sincere, respectful conversation. If you're not a parent, read to your pet. And if you don't have a pet, check out the Library Volunteer stretch assignment in Chapter Nine.

VOLUME

The most clearly enunciated consonants and vowels are useless if they're spoken too quietly. That's why volume and projection are so important.

Voice coaches will tell you that the key to developing a voice that carries is to resonate each sound from your entire body. It should begin in your belly and flow up through your chest. But from my experience, unless you're moonlighting as a singer, investing the time to develop a rich voice is more trouble than it's worth. At least in my case, the payoff was too slow and small to warrant the effort.

So just make sure your volume matches the size and acoustics of whatever room you happen to be in. One trick is to imagine lobbing your words to the audience members about three fourths of the way back. Visualize a streaming rainbow of words arching over those in the front and splashing on your target. If you're reaching people near the back, you're likely reaching everyone else. But don't spit. This is only a visualization.

PACE

Your presentation pace should match your natural speaking pace. The only caveat is that you should speak slowly enough for your audience to keep up, but quickly enough to hold their attention. Don'ttalksofastthatyourwordsruntogether. But at the same time, don't...speak...so...slowly...that...you... sound...like...a...cartoon...turtle. Find some comfortable middle ground that sounds good to your ears.

For extra effectiveness, adjust your pace depending on what you're saying. You can slow down and lower your voice to add a touch of seriousness. Or speed up and raise your voice to indicate urgency or importance. "Please shut the door," can mean fifteen different things, depending on which word I emphasize and how I do it. "Please... shut...*the door,*" emphasizes how much I want the door shut. But so too might yelling the word "SHUT." Varying your pace is just one tool you have at your disposal to convey precisely what you intend.

Last, remember that silence is your friend. The boisterous guests on television news shows have taught us that if our voice isn't filling the air with a constant stream of sound, someone else will fill it for us. However, that's not a worry when you're delivering the typical presentation. The floor is yours—no one's waiting to interrupt. So use pauses to hammer home key points, or to mentally plan your next steps.

If at any time you lose your place, don't panic, apologize or fill the gap with a string of "ums." Calmly reflect, consult your outline if necessary, and begin again. As much stage experience as I have, and as much as I prepare for any given presentation, I still lose my place from time to time and need to regroup. In no case has the silence killed anyone. If anything, my ability to calmly work through the pauses confirmed that I was fully in control, which earned credibility points with my audiences and boosted my confidence. If you've prepared, your memory will eventually kick in. Trust it, and view those unplanned pauses as welcome breaks.

Key Takeaways

➲ JFK and Arnold didn't hide their accents, and neither should **you**

➲ If you're a natural mumbler, practice tongue twisters or read **aloud**

➲ Speak **up** so your audience can hear you

➲ If you lose your place, calmly **consult** your notes and begin again—no sweat

Chapter Six

If You Must
Use a Script...

In their classic and definitive work, *The Art of Public Speaking*, Dale Carnegie and J. Berg Esenwein declare reading a scripted speech the lowest form of public speaking. If those masters of the craft considered scripts a bad thing, that should be warning enough for the rest of us! But this is independently good advice.

Scripted speeches are in most cases unnecessarily stuffy—only appropriate on a handful of very formal occasions, such as political rallies or funerals. But even then, a politician or eulogizer is likely to come across as more competent and sincere if he or she speaks from memory and elaborates on his or her points in the moment.

Your goal as a speaker should be to understand your material well enough to be able to explain it on the fly, using only an outline or a few notes. However, depending on your level of experience, I know the temptation to use a script may be great. I used scripts in my first public speaking class in college, and read scripted lecture notes from PowerPoint slides when I first started teaching.

So while I join Carnegie and Esenwein in encouraging you to avoid them at all costs, there's no shame in using a script when you're a public speaking novice. Just commit to letting them go as soon as possible, and in the meantime, if you must use one, the key to doing so well is looking up often, and making sure it's written the way you speak.

For whatever reason, our written voice is a little different from our spoken voice. That is, the way you would describe your weekend plans in an email is probably different from the way you would describe them over the phone. Just open your Sent folder and read your most recent message aloud. Sounds a little awkward when spoken, doesn't it?

Reading your script out loud and revising it as you go is therefore absolutely essential. Be especially mindful of missed contractions. While you might write "it is" and "do not," you probably more naturally say "it's" and "don't."

On the off chance that you'll be using a teleprompter, keep in mind that reading words overlaying a camera lens is an odd and potentially unnerving experience. Luckily there are several free tools available online that will let you practice. Just google "teleprompter practice," paste your script into the tool, select a scroll speed, and have at it.

Even if you're not using a teleprompter, the more you re-hearse, the better you'll understand and anticipate your different sections, and the less you'll need to refer to your notes. As that becomes the case, my advice and challenge is that you trim your paragraphs until you're left with no more than a detailed outline, and finally with only a bulleted list. If you need to use a full script the first few times you present, that's completely fine. But remember that the goal is to eventually leave it at home. You can do it!

Key Takeaways

⮑ Scripts are formal and stuffy, so only use one when you **must**

⮑ Write a script as you **naturally** speak—using contractions, for example

⮑ Go scriptless and you'll appear more **competent** and sincere

Chapter Seven

Involving Your Audience

I always cringe when a presenter begins by saying, "Raise your hand if you've ever [insert something trite]." While their heart is in the right place, most audiences are not interested in playing the Hokey Pokey.

However, finding ways to actively involve your audience is definitely a good idea. If done well, it wins both their respect and attention. But rather than pressuring them to extend their limbs on command, I recommend that you instead invite them to engage in brief but earnest conversation. If you can get them to think—if only just for a moment—they'll be more alert, and more likely to actively reflect on your message rather than passively tuning out.

GIVE THEM SOMETHING TO CHEW ON

For example, whenever I present on political philosophy, it's obligatory to include the work of twentieth century American philosopher John Rawls. Rather than simply telling the audience Rawls's conclusions, I'll lay out his arguments and invite them to think through his reasoning process for themselves.

Rawls was concerned by the fact that our personal perspective tends to shape our political views. That is, poor white males, on average, tend to favor policies that benefit poor white males; rich black females, on average, tend to favor policies that benefit rich black females, and similar generalizations can be said of people of every socio-economic group. Whether a person thinks they're enlightened or not, political reasoning would seem to be nothing more than a game where citizens promote their narrow self-interests—everyone trying to get the most for themselves and no one seeking objective justice.

But what if we didn't know what our interests were? Imagine if scientists could alter our brains, causing us to temporarily forget our race, sex, wealth, intelligence, religious affiliation, hobbies, handicaps, passions and the like. Might that allow us to transcend our perspectives and think through political questions in an unbiased way? If so, what sort of government and what sort of policies would we endorse?

Just as I put the question to my audiences, I'll put the question to you! If you didn't know if you were rich and famous or broke and homeless, what level of taxation and what sorts of public programs would you support? If you didn't know your race, what sort of non-discrimination laws would you support? If you didn't know if you were a man or a woman, how would you think through laws concerning sexual equality? If you didn't know if you owned a dozen rifles or had never shot one in your life, how would you think through firearms policy?

Of course, I could jump right into Rawls's conclusions. I could explain how he thinks citizens behind a "Veil of Ignorance" would demand something similar to the United States Bill of Rights. Or how he thinks they would tolerate wealth inequality, but only if it somehow benefitted the least well-off group. Or I could present the common objection that Rawls is assuming people blocked from knowing anything about themselves would be risk averse.

But by allowing the audience to come to their own conclusions, they're much more engaged, much more alert, and much more likely to come away with a deeper understanding and appreciation of Rawls's views. Whether they agree with his conclusions is inconsequential. I simply want them to understand his arguments well enough to form their own views, which is much more likely to happen if I talk *with* them, rather than *at* them.

HAVE THEM PRACTICE

Similarly, if your topic happens to concern an activity, find a way for your audience to practice it on the spot. For example, when I present on public speaking, I'll have the crowd pair off and give their partners a thirty-second talk on who they are, where they're from, and what they do for fun. Once they're finished, I'll combine the groups of two into groups of four and repeat the process—each person taking turns to stand and address their four-person group. Then we'll expand to groups of eight, then groups of sixteen, and by the time I'm ready for folks to come to the front of the room and speak to the entire audience, it's much less intimidating.

Also, when I give presentations on personal defense, I always explain the importance of awareness and avoidance, emphasize that the goal is to escape to safety, and demonstrate a few techniques. But it's not until the audience is actively involved that they really begin to learn. Whether it's sharing their own brushes with violence, or practicing the Urban Honey Badger (by the way, that's a callback—and this callback to callbacks is a meta-callback), they learn far more and have a far better time when they're actually doing rather than simply listening.

Whatever your topic, find creative ways to actively involve your audience. Engage them mentally and/or physically, and they'll be much more likely to actively listen, and you'll be much more likely to successfully transfer ideas from your mind into theirs. Just remember, no Hokey Pokey!

Key Takeaways

➲ An **involved** audience is an attentive audience

➲ **Engage** the crowd mentally with good questions, or physically with relevant actions (no Hokey Pokey!)

➲ Political philosophy is **cool**

Chapter Eight

USING
TECHNOLOGY

Whether it's a microphone, a projector, a telephone or a computer, the key to effectively using technology as a public speaker is to think of your equipment as a simple extension of yourself.

There are few things more frustrating as a speaker than technology problems, so anytime you have the opportunity, do a complete dry run of your presentation on site, connecting all equipment to ensure it works. Confirm that the projector is compatible with your laptop, that the speakers are loud enough, that the microphone works, etc.

Doing a dry run not only ensures your technology will work, it makes the actual presentation feel more familiar, and you a more relaxed presenter as a result. Ideally you'll do this a day or two ahead of time so your subconscious mind can reinforce that familiarity while you're asleep. But if all you can do is show up an hour before show time, that's much better than not doing a dry run at all.

USING A MICROPHONE

Using a microphone takes some getting used to. If it's a corded hand-held mic, one of your hands will be constantly occupied, and you'll have to watch out for the cord to keep from tripping. If it's a stationary lectern mic, you won't be able to walk around as you might otherwise prefer. So if you're not used to using one, it's important to rehearse and to rehearse as you plan to deliver.

If you know that you'll be anchored to a lectern, turn a cardboard box upside down on a table, stab a pencil in the top, and pretend it's your grand stage. If you know you'll be using a corded hand-held mic, practice with a hairdryer. Just don't do any of this in public.

Also, one tip I learned from the comedy pros about using a corded mic is to avoid the temptation to wrap excess cord around your hand. Doing so is distracting to both you and the audience, so just let that cord lie.

Finally, if you get a wireless lapel mic, you shouldn't have to change much of anything. They're very sensitive, so you should be able to speak normally. Let whoever's running the audio equipment adjust the volume if need be.

THE JOYS OF POWERPOINT

The key to effectively using presentation software such as PowerPoint, Keynote (Mac only), Impress (free), GoogleDocs (free), and Prezi (potentially dizzying—use with caution) is remembering that it's an aid, not a crutch or a replacement.

While you and your slides should work together symbiotically, the main focus should remain on you and your message.

The visualizations should illustrate and amplify your ideas—they shouldn't replace you. If they can replace you, this means you're probably using too much text, and everyone might be better off if you submitted a written report instead. So PowerPoint tip #1: Don't put everything in your "slide deck," as they call it in DC.

Second, when it comes to animation, use your own judgment as to what best fits your purpose and style. I very rarely use text that spins or glows, or slides that transition by swirling off the screen. When I click, I want the new slide to simply replace the old, and for the bullets to simply appear when I need them. Much more than that seems to come across as amateurish, at least when it's coming from me. However, if your topic is extra lighthearted, or spinning text fits who you are, by all means, spin away!

Third, fewer slides are better than more, and pictures trump text. PowerPoint is a visual aid—it should add to and reinforce what you're saying, not repeat it verbatim in written form. As you prepare your slides, googling key terms and clicking "Images" is an easy and effective way to find relevant visuals, though be sure to check the copyright law and/or give the photographers due credit. Keep your bullets to phrases or short sentence fragments, and use them just as you would an outline—not as a script, but as something to keep you on track.

Last, if you're going to use PowerPoint a lot, it's worth investing in a remote so you can transition through your slides from afar. The basic models will do—no need for a laser pointer unless you'll be giving briefings at the Pentagon.

PRESENTING REMOTELY

When presenting to a remote audience, whether via teleconference, LiveMeeting, GoToMeeting, webcam or some mix, the challenge of holding their attention increases tenfold. It's tough enough for some audience members to resist the temptation to constantly check their BlackBerry/Droid/iPhone/Whatever when you can see them. Imagine all the multitasking they're doing when you're not in the same room!

However, your job as remote presenter is actually easier in some ways, for you'll have resources at your fingertips you likely wouldn't in front of a live audience. And unless you'll be on camera, you won't have to worry quite as much about your silent message. You should still prepare a clear presentation and rehearse, but you won't need to master your material quite as well as if you were delivering your presentation in person—you can always pull up reference materials, refer back to your notes, and have a timer in front of you to ensure you stay on schedule.

Apart from taking advantage of all the resources you can use out of your audience's view, you can maximize the effectiveness of any remote presentation by doing three additional things.

The first is to consider explicitly asking your audience to give you their full attention, and promising to put on a good show in return. Build this into your opening, and do it in a friendly, inviting way. Explain that you've taken the time to research your topic and develop a quality presentation, and hint at what's in it for them—how what you're about to teach will improve their lives. Then agree to end ten minutes early if they promise to ignore the distractions on their end, and voila!—their anti-multitasking willpower just increased tenfold.

The second is that it's especially important with remote presentations to find ways to involve your audience early and often. I once gave a webinar on business ethics to a mixed group of human resource specialists, website designers, and managers of different sorts. To hook them early, I began with what philosophers and attorneys know as the classic trolley scenario.

You see a runaway trolley about to crash into and kill a group of five innocent people. However, you happen to be near a lever that can divert the trolley onto another track, sparing the five, but surely killing one innocent person on the second track. What should you do? Stand by and allow the original five to die, or flip the switch, effectively killing a person who would otherwise survive?

Rather than using the presentation software to take a poll, I asked the open-ended question, "What do you think a person in this situation should do, and why?" This led to a brief conversation on the differences among psychological predictability, legal permissibility, and moral rightness, and opened the participants' minds in a way that a monologue never would have. It set the tone for the rest of the presentation, and when I got to a case study involving employee privacy, I had no trouble getting folks to discuss.

If you're especially worried about audience engagement, ask a question and then call on attendees by name. Once you've called on a couple, everyone will be on their toes so they don't get caught dozing.

Last, practice with your technology and make sure you're using it well. If you're on a call, speak clearly and directly into the mic. If you're using a webcam, don't forget about your silent message, and make sure the camera is capturing your face and torso—not just the top of your hair and ceiling.

Key Takeaways

⮕ PowerPoint is a visual **aid**—less text, more pictures

⮕ Engaging a remote audience is **doubly** important

⮕ If you practice with a **pretend** mic, don't let anyone see you!

Chapter Nine

LESS READING, MORE DOING

When beginning a new project, smart house painters will practice their brush stroke somewhere inconspicuous, like under the back deck. Once they're warmed up, then they'll paint the high-visibility areas, like the front porch. Similarly, top college football programs will often schedule low-ranked opponents early in the season as a way to give their freshman some experience before the big games later in the year.

I'd like to give you the chance to develop as a speaker in a similar fashion: slowly, beginning with simple low-stakes opportunities, where it doesn't really matter if you mess up, and progressing through opportunities with increasing complexity and importance. You can adopt the plan below wholesale, customize it to your situation, or just jump right into high-stakes presentations. It's completely your call.

The only thing that isn't optional is whether you present. The time to begin is now. Not after you finish the book; not when the stars align—now. No more delays. No more excuses.

We'll begin with simple, easy, confidence-building activities that are fully doable right now, today, regardless of your level of experience. These "quick wins" may seem insignificant, but depending on how much public speaking you've done, they could prove to be indispensable building blocks.

Then we'll branch into opportunities that are slightly more formal, with slightly larger crowds, slightly more complex topics, and slightly higher stakes. You'll find the step from "quick wins" into "stretch assignments" fun and exciting, for by the time you get there, you'll definitely be ready for a bigger challenge. You may even be ready right now.

Finally, with multiple live presentations under your belt, you'll be ready for "show time"—the reason you're doing all this work. What this entails for you is only bound by your imagination. So aim high—no reason to settle for office briefs if you're ready for theatre.

Quick Wins

Low-risk and to a small audience, quick wins are what their title implies: fast and easy ways to build your public speaking experience and confidence. This is super simple stuff, and if you're a novice, this is a wonderful place to begin your public speaking journey. No more procrastination; no more excuses. Decide to dominate, and let's go.

1. Your Story

Develop, revise, rehearse and find opportunities to tell others your unique story. You're the author of this story, so make your personal past, present and future a pleasure to both hear and tell.

For example, two important events happened to me soon after getting out of the Air Force: I got laid off from a job (which gave me motivation to turn a part time business into a fulltime business), and I started dating my sister's best friend (whom I wed three years later). Both events were important, yet people always seem to prefer to hear the love story. And just as importantly, I always prefer to tell it. Make your story a happy one as well.

Once your story is ready, rehearse, and put yourself in a set-ting where people will be invited to introduce themselves. Have a rough outline in your head, preferably ordered chronologically, and unpack it as you go. This exercise is not only great public speaking practice, it may even help you bet-ter understand where you've been, where you are, and where you're going.

2. Checkout Speech

If you're in need of networking advice, Susan RoAne's *How to Work a Room* is an excellent resource, chock-full of practical and effective tips.

For example, anytime you find yourself among strangers at a networking opportunity, seek out and introduce yourself to people who are alone, and especially people who are alone and look uncomfortable. Why? They probably don't know anyone either, and are therefore likely to appreciate and welcome your company.

RoAne recommends that before you try using her tips at a presidential dinner, you should practice on a captive audience who is likely to welcome friendly conversation—such as a grocery store clerk.

However, rather than simply making small talk, your assignment here is to actually covertly deliver a prepared presentation. Talk about something of mutual interest, such as the sale on cucumbers, or maybe the weather. Or swap recipes. "Have you tried this chili mix? My mother always added cumin and…" is a great way to start. Then roll into your prepared sub-points on achieving the perfect combination of spice and cheese. Or convince them to form a union and overthrow their corporate overlords. Make it fun!

The more depth and complexity you build into your check-out speech, the better. But for now, just get it out. The point is to get a little experience in following a mental outline, and to build a little confidence in the process.

STRETCH ASSIGNMENTS

With several quick wins under your belt, now's the time to increase your audience size and up the stakes. But not too much!

3. Library Volunteer

As the title implies, this assignment involves volunteering at your local library. If yours already holds weekly story times for kids, ask if you can help with the next one. If it doesn't, volunteer to organize and host one next Saturday. (That's right—I said *next Saturday.* No excuses!)

Preparing is easy. You're just going to read a children's book aloud. But be sure to practice holding the book at an angle that will allow you to see the words and the kids to see the pictures—this is one of the few times it's actually preferable to read from a script.

Once you're comfortable with the basic storyline and have read it aloud a couple of times, try your hand at bringing the characters to life. Put some bass into the Big Bad Wolf's huffs and puffs. And make sure the troll under that bridge actually sounds like a troll, and the Billy Goats Gruff have voices that match their varied ages and sizes.

I used to read children's stories to third and fourth graders as part of a Philosophy for Kids program, and the experience did wonders for my growth as a speaker. Although kids are a very forgiving audience so long as your story is good, they're also very honest, and their attention spans are notoriously short.

As I learned, presenting to kids really makes a speaker work on eye contact, voice inflection, movement, and general audience engagement. Plus, if you mess up, who cares—they're just a bunch of kids. So give it a try! It's sure to be very rewarding, for both you and your audience.

4. Big Idea

Think of a way to improve something that will need the cooperation of others. It could be at work, at home, in the community, among friends—your choice.

Once you've identified your big idea, develop, revise and practice a presentation, and schedule a time to pitch it. In fact, schedule a time to pitch your idea first, then develop your presentation. Having that date on the calendar will ensure you actually get it done.

This presentation will have a very basic structure: 1) Here's the issue background, 2) Here's the problem I'd like to address, 3) Here's my suggested solution, and 4) Here's why this solution is better than others.

Since this is only a stretch assignment, you can make your presentation as formal or as informal as you like. Just remember that the point is twofold: to communicate a valuable solution and grow as a speaker.

5. Family Prayer

If you and your family happen to be religious, prepare a brief, simple, but sincere prayer for your next gathering, and recite it before the meal. If you and your family happen to not be religious, same assignment—just keep your eyes open and address your loved ones directly rather than talking to God.

If you're having trouble finding inspiration, talk about how blessed you are to have one another, how grateful you are for the food, and how eager you are to eat it. You are eager to eat it, aren't you?

SHOW TIME

You've done enough studying and practicing. It's show time!

6. Open Mic

Ah, open mic night at the local comedy club. Here we go—it's time for a real audience, a real microphone, and some real expectations! But to lessen that pressure, I'm giving you permission to do something typically considered an unforgivable comedic sin. Rather than spending the *enormous* amount of time it takes to author, refine, and perfect a quality original routine, just copy some jokes from the Internet.

However, you have to announce upfront that the jokes you're telling aren't your own, and give credit to the original author or performer. Just explain that you're not there to become the next Jerry Seinfeld, but because "Professor Matt" told you doing open mics was a great way to grow as a public speaker.

I think you'll find it a very rewarding experience. Normal public speaking is already fun, but there's nothing like making a room full of people burst into physical joy with your words. That instant and emphatic group approval is satisfying on an almost instinctual level—I suspect even if you're delivering someone else's material.

If you happen to like it and catch the comedy bug, check out Greg Dean's *Step by Step to Stand-Up Comedy*, or Judy Carter's *Stand-Up Comedy: The Book*. Both are excellent places for aspiring comedians to begin.

7. Why You Picked Up the Book

You picked up this book with some idea of when, where and how you'd like to speak publicly. You didn't just think, "I doubt I'll ever want to give a presentation...but why don't I read this entire book anyway!" No; you had something in mind, and whatever that was, by the time you've read this far and completed the growth assignments above (or something like them), you're ready to tackle your original goal.

Remember, conditions will never, ever be completely perfect. At some point you have to just get up there and do it. (Skip ahead to the Roosevelt quote in Chapter Thirteen for extra inspiration.)

So what if you're not perfect? So what if you're not even excellent! There will be more opportunities to shine, and you'll improve as you go. So don't procrastinate on this one. All the time you've spent studying and practicing is wasted if you never get out there and do the presentation you were aiming for all along. Take that first small step toward making it a reality. Today.

8. Go Bigger!

Whatever speaking engagement you had in mind when you picked up the book, I'm sure it was originally impressive. But with all you've learned, and all you're doing, don't you think it's a little too easy for a person like you? I do. Now dream bigger.

And don't just dream, for dreams without a plan remain dreams, and plans without action remain plans. Dream, plan, act, *realize*.

Key Takeaways

➲ **Your Story**: Author and share a happy autobiography.

➲ **Checkout Speech**: Grow as a speaker as you brighten your cashier's day.

➲ **Library Volunteer**: Read books to kids. *The Giving Tree* is a good one!

➲ **Big Idea**: You have an idea to improve something. Tell us about it.

➲ **Family Prayer**: Be ready for Thanksgiving with an earnest prayer.

➲ **Open Mic**: Visit your local comedy club. No pressure to be funny—just practicing.

➲ **Why You Picked Up the Book**: Whatever presentation you had in mind when you started reading, go do it!

➲ **Go Bigger**: And don't just dream—act!

Chapter Ten

THE COMMITMENT TO GET BETTER

Successful CEOs study past sales, anticipate technological developments and changing customer needs, and redesign and market accordingly. Successful politicians study the policy platforms and pitches that have won elections in the past, gauge current voter preferences, and implement campaigns to match.

You can and should do the same as a growing public speaker. Background study, general preparation, and practice are essential. But if you want to accelerate your improvement, analyze every speaking opportunity for ways to get better.

TWO CASE STUDIES

Here are self-analyses of two of my own presentations. For the first, I was asked by my director to brief our Associate Deputy Assistant Secretary (ADAS) on the vision and values portion of our service's strategic plan. Main upshot? I found the experience more nerve-wracking than expected, which taught me some important lessons about preparing exactly as I'll deliver, but reaffirmed my ability to work through bouts of nervousness.

ADAS Brief

<u>Preparation</u>: Drafted presentation slides and talking points on Wednesday. Rehearsed solo six times Thursday and three times Friday.

<u>Monday Morning Dress Rehearsal</u>: Sat around a large conference table with half a dozen colleagues—felt fine going in, but heart sped up as my turn to speak approached. By the time I began speaking my heart was racing, so much so that my voice quivered. Not sure why!

<u>Monday Afternoon Real Thing</u>: Sat around a small conference table with same colleagues—not nearly as nervous as during dry run, but failed to fully elaborate on key points as planned. Interruptions from ADAS threw off delivery.

Analysis:

Observation A: The dress rehearsal really helped. Taking the time to practice around a similar table with my presentation partners made the real thing much easier, especially since I have lots of experience presenting solo while standing, but very little experience presenting as part of a group sitting down.

Lessons:

1. Do dress rehearsal every time—better to have first-time foul-ups during practice than the real thing.

Observation B: Presenting sitting down felt very awkward—especially around a small table in a small room. And while I practiced several times beforehand, almost every time I was standing up.

Lessons:

1. Practice exactly as you will speak, whether that's seated, standing, using a lectern, not using a lectern, with a mic, without a mic, etc.
2. Volunteer for more seated speaking opportunities.

Observation C: I got much more nervous than expected. Maybe it was because I'm relatively new to the office and the culture? Or because I didn't fully appreciate the background of my presentation? Or because I was infected by the nervousness of others?

Lessons:

1. Despite your newness and the hierarchy, remember that you're pretty awesome—never let the

perceived opinion of others impact your self-esteem.

2. Know thy material—be sure to fully understand the material you're responsible for presenting, including background context.

3. Be the Fonz—strive to serve as a role model of cool and calm rather than letting the nervousness of others drag you down.

As you can see, some things went well, and some things didn't. By reflecting on both, I was able to illuminate lessons learned, which will enable me to adjust my preparation for next time, and ultimately become an even better speaker.

I gave that ADAS presentation on a Monday afternoon. Here's an analysis of a welcome speech I gave the following Saturday at American University, as host of the inaugural Washington DC Area High School Ethics Bowl. This was a side project I had worked on for several months, and one that was in jeopardy of not succeeding at several stages. But by the time the bowl arrived, it was clear it would be a success—it was just a matter of execution.

DC Ethics Bowl

<u>Preparation</u>: Spent most of my free time the week prior confirming volunteer participation, selecting cases, printing ma-

terials, and otherwise handling logistics. I didn't sketch an official outline until late Friday, which I briefly rehearsed while getting ready the next morning, and again on my way to the event. Also, spent time self-coaching on the way in, deciding that not only would my opening speech go well, but so too would the entire event; I visualized how much fun the participants would have, and how satisfied I'd feel later that afternoon, after months of preparation, with a wildly successful bowl complete.

<u>Show Time</u>: The joy of seeing the bowl come together and my focus on greeting guests prevented my nerves from acting up beforehand. The crowd was very positive and enthusiastic—so much so that my opening line, "Welcome to the inaugural Washington DC Area High School Ethics Bowl," was met with cheers and applause! That unexpected response created a wave of enthusiasm that carried me through my main points. Though my transitions could have been smoother, and I forgot the names of a couple of people I intended to thank, it was overall a very successful presentation.

Analysis:

Observation A: I was very comfortable presenting solo, standing, and being able to walk around. Felt like I was back in the college classroom.

Lessons:

1. I should always attempt to present under these conditions.

Observation B: The audience's enthusiasm fueled my confidence.

Lessons:

1. Always present on happy topics to happy people!
2. When above not possible, expect audience to be happy, and anytime they're obviously not (throwing tomatoes), imagine that they're happy—should have a similar effect.

Observation C: Forgot a few key names. Whoops!

Lessons:

1. Use notes for unfamiliar key info—much better to read a coach's name than to have to ask the audience.

As you can see, I have room for improvement! Couldn't believe I forgot those names... But overall it was a huge success, and I learned some valuable lessons in the process.

It takes extra time and effort to reflect on your performances and develop an improvement plan. But it really works. Six months after that ADAS speech, I was back in the same room, this time presenting to the ADAS's boss and team of service directors—what should have been a much more intimidating audience. But in part thanks to lessons I learned from the first time around, I'm proud to say I felt great going in, and absolutely *nailed* that presentation. I had only rehearsed once, but it was sitting down, and this time I really understood the topic. Lesson: practice exactly as you'll perform and know thy material!

If my experience isn't enough, look to top athletes for confirmation that performance analysis is worth the trouble. Win or lose, most spend the entire first working day after a game watching film. They study what they did poorly, but also what they did well. Then they scout their next opponent, come up with a customized plan to correct their weaknesses and build on their strengths, and get to work. If you're serious about getting better, at most anything, practice is essential. But developing a performance improvement plan will get you there even faster.

Key Takeaways

➲ Practice **exactly** as you'll perform

➲ Have notes on **standby** for key details

➲ Mitigate your weaknesses and **build** on your strengths

➲ Matt remembers the **Fonz** (Do you?)

Chapter Eleven

BE THYSELF

Had I been born ten years earlier, I might have grown out my hair and headbanged my way through high school. Had I been born ten years later, I might have bought some glow sticks and a pacifier, and raved in caves...whatever that means.

As it happens, I came of age during the mid-90s, which, for better or worse, was at the height of the gangsta rap phenomenon. As a small-town country boy, the rebellious lyrics of Dr. Dre, Eazy E and Snoop Dogg portrayed a seemingly glamorous alternative to the slow-paced small town. I bought into their narrative, changing my dress and attitude to match, oblivious for a time just how silly farm boys look in sagging pants.

THE IMPORTANCE OF BEING THYSELF

We've all pretended to be someone we're not at one time or another—perhaps to impress someone we considered worth impressing, or to live up to imagined expectations, or just because doing so seemed cool at the time. Most often our insincerity happens in little ways. We force a smile, nervously laugh at an unfunny joke, suppress or change our accent, pretend to like things we don't, or to know about things of which we're actually ignorant. But as we all know in our hearts, it's far more peaceful and satisfying to simply be yourself.

As hip hop mogul Russell Simmons explains in *Do You! 12 Laws to Access the Power In You to Achieve Happiness and Success*, being yourself also gives you a competitive advantage. There's only one person with your unique perspective, personality and talents. Try to be someone else and they'll always win. But commit in all things to "do you" and it's you who's unbeatable. You enjoy an absolute monopoly on your unique brand, so exploit it for all its worth.

As a speaker, being yourself enables an otherwise unattainable rapport with your audience. In a world saturated with dishonest advertising and manipulative "reality" television stars, people long for sincerity and instantly respect those who have it. Conversely, people can spot insincerity a mile away, and once they see it, it's almost impossible to regain their trust.

Plus, public speaking isn't hard, but it does take some degree of concentration. Just as a computer slows when it's running several programs at once, our brain can't devote 100% to delivering a top-notch presentation when it's also trying to maintain a fake identity.

Being your true self is an effortless, liberating, and energizing experience. If you're old enough to remember *Cheers*, think of how great Norm, Cliff and Frasier felt when they were able to drop all the pretense and just be themselves at the bar. Of course, they were alcoholics...so maybe this isn't the best example.

But reflect for a moment and I bet you can think of a certain place among a certain group of people where you feel most in tune with your true self. A place where you don't feel the need to mimic the West Coast rapper. Where you can simply *do you.*

If it's been a long time since you've experienced that feeling, now's the time to feel it again. And if that safe place is too far away to visit or gone completely, you'll have to imagine it for now, and begin creating a new one wherever you happen to be. One of your goals as a person—not just as a speaker—should be to let your true self shine brighter and more often. The world is full of enough fakery. Do us all a favor. *Be thyself.*

JEET KUNE DO YOU

The importance of being yourself applies to all you do as a public speaker, not just to your delivery. Whether you're brainstorming, organizing, revising or rehearsing—think about what feels right and seems to work best for you.

This is the approach martial arts legend Bruce Lee used to develop his own system, Jeet Kune Do. Lee studied many styles under many masters, but never deferred to authority or tradition when deciding which techniques to adopt, and which to forget. Rather, he tested each for himself, and only internalized those that actually worked.

This is the approach I've used during my growth as a public speaker, and as a public speaking coach. I've studied the experts, tested various presenting and coaching techniques, and only kept the best of the best.

However, not every tip resonates with every person. The best way for *you* to prepare, practice and deliver a presentation, or conquer nervousness, or anything, is partially a function of who you are. I therefore qualify everything I'm teaching with the caveat that you should always defer to firsthand testing.

Your personal perspective and experience trump any expert's advice—including mine. So while I encourage you to give every good idea a fair try, be sure to customize the way you develop and deliver presentations according to what works for you. I suspect Lee taught his students the same thing.

DISCOVERING YOUR STAGE SELF

As you work to discover and refine your authentic stage self, keep in mind that it's simply one version of the sincere you. I'm a slightly different person when I'm wrestling with my kids, discussing theology, buying groceries, cheering at a big football game, eating at a family reunion, or watching a movie with my wife. This doesn't mean there's no real, authentic Matt underneath. It just means the real authentic Matt varies slightly depending on where he happens to be and what he happens to be doing. Trust me, this is a good thing—you don't want Football Game Matt at the family reunion!

As you might expect, there's a public speaking Matt as well. I had very little public speaking experience before college, and I can remember dealing with nervousness in my first public speaking class by faking a huge grin during my first presentation. Apart from making it difficult to speak, my smile was confusing to the audience. If my memory serves me, it was on Oklahoma City bomber Timothy McVeigh—not a smiling matter.

As soon as I sat down I realized how silly I must have looked, how ineffective I'd been, and how terrible being fake felt. So I vowed then and there to always speak with sobriety and sincerity—to be myself, whatever that self happened to be.

Over time I've developed a public speaking voice that's true to the real me, but tailored for the stage in light of my goals, strengths and personality. Anytime I catch myself trying to sound smarter, fancier, funnier, more interesting or more upbeat than I actually am, I try to remember that I'll be a much more effective presenter, and ultimately a much happier person, if I'm simply me.

Discovering your public speaking self will come with practice, but you might begin by revisiting those times and places you've felt most like your true self—especially as a communicator. I happened to notice that I was especially articulate and felt especially confident anytime I welcomed a new person onto a team, whether it was a new kid at school, a new student in Jiu Jitsu class, or a new colleague at work. So now when I give presentations, I try to think of my audience members as new guys and gals I'm attempting to bring up to speed. The approachable, knowledgeable, avuncular personality that naturally flows not only feels sincere, but seems to best capture a crowd's attention and open their minds for the ideas I have to convey—a win-win for everyone.

So before you can *do* you, you have to *find* you—or at least find your authentic stage self. And perhaps the best and only way to do that is through introspection and experience. You won't know what feels right in front of a crowd until you've been up there a few times, so if you're not presenting regularly, now's the time to begin.

AUTHENTIC IMPROVEMENT

Last, I want to clarify that being thyself is consistent with improvement. It doesn't mean you're locked into your upbringing or destined to repeat old habits, or that if you're not the same person at eighty that you were at eighteen you're somehow fake.

Rather, being yourself means you are your own author, and that no one defines you but you. It means you take the initiative to think about the person you've been, the person you are, and the person you want to become. It means that you're not satisfied to simply copy a template established by someone else, or coast through life without pushing yourself to become more than you are. It means that you're committed to finding, embodying, and optimizing your true self, which changes over time and is completely consistent with improvement.

Take a moment to reflect on what your ideal stage self looks like. What expression do you have on your face? What are you wearing? How are you standing? How do you sound? How do you feel? How are you interacting with your audience?

Once you have a clear vision in mind, go ahead and be that person! If you can see how your ideal public speaking self moves, sounds and presents, you can become them. Keep that in mind throughout the entire presentation development and delivery process. And remember that you're a work in progress. Being yourself is fully consistent with improving, not just as a speaker, but in all areas of your life.

Key Takeaways

➲ Audiences love **sincere** speakers

➲ Realizing your ideal self is **consistent** with authenticity

➲ Adopt what works for **you** and forget the rest

Chapter Twelve

MINDSET
REVISITED

In Chapter Two we covered the importance of releasing negative thoughts, of amplifying positive thoughts, and of FM-AC. But developing and maintaining a proper mindset is relevant for much more than conquering nervousness.

How you respond to challenges and setbacks will impact whether you flounder or flourish, both as a growing public speaker and as a person. Further, the standard to which you hold yourself and your work will impact the volume and quality of your accomplishments.

Simply reading these words proves that you're no slacker, so that isn't an issue. But if you've ever been guilty of perfectionism, that's something we need to address. For while Voltaire was right that the perfect is the enemy of good, I consider both the perfect and the good our mutual enemies, and the excellent our mutual friend.

IT AIN'T A GRAND PIANO

"It ain't a grand piano." That's the phrase Rita Emmett, author of *The Procrastinator's Handbook: Mastering the Art of Doing It Now*, tells us carpenters repeat anytime they catch themselves fretting over minor flaws when doing typical carpentry.

It's appropriate to spend enormous amounts of time choosing the right wood, measuring, re-measuring, cutting, re-cutting, sanding, re-sanding—ensuring everything is *just right*—when you're making a grand piano, for grand pianos are works of art. But when you're building a bookshelf, it's foolish to waste time and effort attempting to perfect something that doesn't require or deserve it.

Your presentations are not grand pianos. Neither are mine. They're not dingy bookshelves, either. But it's foolish to expect perfection from imperfect creatures, or strive for perfection in projects that don't deserve it. Not only is it pointless, but needlessly frustrating. The smart carpenters know that even when they are making a grand piano, perfection is only an ideal to guide their pursuit of excellence, and not an expected end state.

So aim for excellence instead and you'll be more productive and happier. This applies to everything you do, whether that's organizing your material, practicing your voice projection, tailoring your silent message, or practicing for a particular presentation. You have other goals and obligations that deserve your time and effort as well. Never forget: it ain't a grand piano.

UPROOT SUBCONSCIOUS SABOTAGE

It sounds odd, but sometimes the biggest obstacle to achieving our goals is not a fear of failure, but a subconscious fear of success. While your conscious mind may recognize the benefits of becoming a fantastic public speaker, your subconscious mind may be worried about potential side effects, such as increased responsibility that might come with raised expectations. And when the conscious mind is set on achieving something the subconscious mind isn't ready to embrace, frustration and anxiety are predictable results.

For example, I sometimes got the impression that certain students almost *enjoyed* stage fright—not for its own sake, but for the attention it brought them. They'd lament about how they just *couldn't* give a presentation, and would all but refuse to even try, to the extent that it seemed the attention they got from their phobia had become a source of self-esteem.

However, with a little coaching, encouragement and practice, in every case they excelled as speakers—even those who were initially the most resistant. Once they realized how much better it would feel to be known for their speaking prowess rather than their speaking paralysis, they'd give it an honest try and begin their growth in earnest.

Another example is when I used to open my comedy sets with the following joke:

I go by "Professor Matt" on stage because I really am a professor. And I hate it when people find that out and get all paranoid about their grammar. Look—*I'm* the professor—the pressure's on *me* to be grammatically perfect. Everyone else: *you're free to appear just as ignorant as you actually are.*

This joke made *me* smile, but it often offended my audience. And since it's hard to laugh when you're offended, this wasn't a smart joke to include at all, let alone at the very beginning of a set! So why in the world did I continue to use it until a mentor convinced me to stop?

Although I was never in any danger of being whisked away to Hollywood, I remember thinking how much travel rising comedians had to endure while building their fan base, and how incompatible that seemed with a rich family life. The comics who came to town for the weekend were usually exhausted, having just driven several hundred miles from their last gig, and about to drive several hundred more to their next gig.

As a local club host, while I didn't get paid much, I didn't have to travel either. So even though I really enjoyed the glamour of the spotlight and the thrill of making an audience laugh, I knew it would never be more than a hobby—any career that required long stretches away from my family wasn't a career for me.

So maybe I stuck with that insulting opener for so long because it was my subconscious mind's way of ensuring I never got the opportunity to quit my day job and go on tour. Or maybe my comedic instincts were just terrible!

If you find the idea of public speaking unsettling, maybe the root cause isn't the speaking itself, but some potential consequence of speaking—like a new job that might require an unwanted move, or new responsibilities you're not sure you can handle. Maybe your best friend is a terrible speaker, and you're subconsciously worried that if you improve their jealousy will destroy your relationship. Or maybe your mother still wants you to become a priest, you want to remain an accountant, and your subconscious mind is afraid that if you could speak publicly you'd have one less excuse to avoid seminary.

Whatever the case, one way to defeat subconscious fears is to bring them to the surface and attain what Freud called "insight." Is there anything about being able to speak publicly that might scare or intimidate you?

Give that some thought, and reassure your subconscious by debunking any dubious connections. Nailing a presentation might very well open new doors. But job offers can be refused, your best friend is much more likely to be proud of you than jealous, and Momma's going to pester you about the priesthood regardless.

THINK OF CHALLENGES AS OPPORTUNITIES TO GROW

Students sometimes view college as an obstacle preventing them from attaining a higher paying job. I'll admit that I once viewed it this way. As a result, I resented required classes that didn't seem relevant to my major. "I'm pre-med. There's no medicine in American Literature!"

But as I worked my way through the distribution requirements in the various disciplines, I began to see them not as hoops through which I had to jump, but as opportunities to learn something new. And with the help of many excellent professors, I eventually came to see them not only as chances to learn, but as opportunities to grow as a person.

American Literature wasn't an employment scam for English professors. It was a chance to read some of the most powerful and wisdom-filled stories ever written—wisdom that I could apply to my own life. Western Civilization wasn't just about memorizing and regurgitating historical facts—it was a chance to better understand the political and social world around me. And Intro to Philosophy wasn't pointless poetry about unanswerable questions. It was a fortuitous opportunity to discover a passion for deep, reason-guided thought about big questions that would lead to the switching of majors, and a completely different life trajectory.

To the extent that I looked at my classes as opportunities rather than obstacles, I got more out of them, and when I became a professor myself, I always tried to encourage students to do the same—many of whom were taking my class as one of those dreaded distribution requirements. Those who took my advice always seemed happier, and always seemed to grow more over the course of the semester.

Viewing an otherwise stressful speaking engagement in this way is helpful, both in terms of whether you'll enjoy it, and in terms of how well you'll do. If you thoroughly prepare and expect to do well, you most likely will. But whatever the case, don't be afraid to push yourself to grow. What seems outside of your comfort zone today could be fully within it six months from now. It's all up to you.

THINK OF SETBACKS AS OPPORTUNITIES TO LEARN

About three years after my first public speaking class, where I had grinned my way through that Timothy McVeigh presentation, I was in front of a classroom again—this time as a graduate teaching assistant charged with leading a weekly discussion section for an Intro to Philosophy class. Feeling a little insecure about my grasp of the material, I typed long lectures into PowerPoint, projected them onto the board, and stood at the back of the room (where no one could see me) and read them aloud, word for word.

Three years after that, I was on stage during open mic night at the local comedy club, listening to my first joke completely bomb. I'd read books on comedy, spent hours developing what I thought was an awesome set, and had put what I considered my best material first as all the professionals advised. But somehow the crowd just didn't get my gun safety joke:

The first rule of firearms safety is to never point your weapon at anything you wouldn't want to destroy. And that's really the only firearms safety rule you need...unless you're Godzilla!

Godzilla, of course, wants to destroy everything, so this rule wouldn't give him any guidance, right? Because he's a raging monster, and enjoys destruction, and...oh, forget it.

Those were without doubt some of the lowest points in my public speaking career, but each was a powerful and transformative learning opportunity. By the end of that first public speaking class I'd learned the importance of being myself. By the end of that Intro to Philosophy class I'd realized that my primary job wasn't to prevent the students from discovering what I didn't know, but to teach them the things that I did know. And as I worked through my set that first evening on the comedy stage, I learned the value of perseverance. While the Godzilla joke bombed, the rest of my set did not, and by the time my six minutes were up, I'd earned cheers from the crowd and hearty congrats from my fellow amateur comedians.

Learning opportunities aren't always fun, but I wouldn't be the speaker I am without them. Plus, with every survived mistake, mustering the courage to get up on increasingly bigger stages with increasingly bigger stakes got easier every time.

You're bound to have your own Godzilla moments. But when they happen, don't quit or beat yourself up. Rather, find ways to learn from them. It's all part of the growing process, and they'll make you a much better speaker and a stronger person in the end.

BE SOLUTION-ORIENTED

Top business schools teach MBA students on day one that "No business plan survives first contact with the customer." And it was the iconic boxer, Mike Tyson, who once said, "Everybody has a plan until they get punched in the mouth."

Luckily, public speaking isn't as unpredictable as business or as violent as boxing. Only occasionally will anything out of the ordinary go wrong, and almost never will an audience member punch you in the mouth. *Especially if you avoid those face tattoos!*

However, if you speak often and long enough, you'll eventually run into some sort of unexpected trouble. After these experiences are over, I of course recommend using them as learning opportunities. But as they're happening, and while you can still do something about them, the key is to be solution-oriented.

For example, a friend who works at the Department of Defense was recently briefing a manager in her chain of command on issues involving encryption technology. The topic was a little complex, and the manager just wasn't getting it. But rather than asking my friend for clarification or repeating back to her what she thought was being said, the manager responded by putting her face in her hands and saying, "I'll come back to this next week—I'm just too busy right now."

My friend was at a complete loss. She'd studied. She'd prepared. She'd practiced. But her audience was frustrated and unreceptive, apparently unwilling to meet her halfway. She reluctantly agreed to reschedule the presentation and try again. But could she have done anything better? Perhaps she could have tried the following approach:

If it turns out we really do need to reschedule, I'm happy to come back. But since we're here and have our schedules blocked off, let's give this one more shot. This time I'll make it more of a conversation than a lecture. And maybe if I can better understand what is clear, I can better understand what isn't clear, and we can work together to fill in the gaps. Cool?

Maybe the manager was having a bad day and wouldn't have been open to the idea. But the point is that my friend had options that were more attractive than rescheduling, and she should have explored them. Of course, I've not always handled setbacks so well either.

I remember giving a talk to the philosophy department late one Friday afternoon. Our football team was scheduled to play the Air Force Academy the next day, and right in the middle of my presentation a squadron of low-flying jets buzzed campus—apparently a pre-game tactic used by Air Force brass to intimidate opposing teams.

Those planes weren't just loud. *They physically shook the building.* And though I tried to talk on through it, there was no way I could have held a flight crew's attention—let alone an audience of philosophers. It would have been much better if I had paused, acknowledged the harassing aircraft, and began again once the pilots had had their fun.

It was a good learning experience nonetheless. While the noise may have intimidated the faculty, it only angered our team, who took out their frustration on the Falcons the next day in the form of a victory!

Three years later, I did a little better when I walked onto the comedy club stage and found a dead mic. There I was, the center of attention for roughly 150 paying customers who'd just been whipped into a comedic frenzy by the intro video the club played at the beginning of each show, and my one piece of essential technology was failing.

With the stage lights amplifying my every expression, I'm sure the audience could see my eyes widen and my face redden as my excitement quickly turned to fear. But rather than stalling or running away, I put the mic back in its stand, moved it to the side, took a deep breath, and began my monologue as per usual—only using extra volume to ensure folks in the back could hear.

In retrospect, adding a quip about the cheap owners and the electric bill might have been even better. But I was able to work through the equipment failure because I immediately focused on solutions. Luckily, Troy the sound man/engineer/bouncer rushed to the stage and had the mic working in no time, and when he gave the thumbs up I calmly retrieved it from the stand without missing a beat.

The point of the noisy jets and dead mic stories isn't to make you think problems are inevitable. They're not. I've spoken on hundreds of occasions, and those are the only negative instances worth mentioning that I recall. The vast majority of the time, technology works as it should and nearby planes maintain an appropriate altitude.

The point instead is that on the rare occasion that hiccups do occur, just shift into solution mode and do whatever it takes to overcome them. If the power goes out, you can get mad and curse the electric company—or you can use your cellphone as a flashlight and continue until maintenance comes to the rescue. If the building catches fire, you can scream and run in a circle—or you can coordinate an orderly evacuation and continue your talk in the parking lot.

You should expect things to go very well—not only because both positive and negative prophecies tend to self-fulfill, but because from my experience, genuine setbacks are rare. So long as you've prepared and practiced, you'll do fine. And on the rare occasion that things do go wrong, take a deep breath, focus on the solution, and just press on through.

Key Takeaways

➲ Aim for **excellence**, not perfection

➲ Ensure **subconscious** worries aren't undermining your conscious goals

➲ Use challenges to **grow** and setbacks to learn

➲ In all things, focus on the **fix**, not the problem

Chapter Thirteen

TELL THEM WHAT YOU'VE TOLD THEM

My goal in this book has been to give you both the know-how and the motivation to become the best public speaker you're capable of becoming. Toward that end, we've covered a lot—from the mind-body loop and the Urban Honey Badger, to the importance of consciously tailoring your silent message and logically arranging your ideas, to the essential keys of knowing your material, practicing, being yourself, and maintaining a positive attitude.

Along the way I've tried to hammer home the basic truth that public speaking is simply a form of communication—a mere matter of transferring ideas in your head into the heads of your audience members. Nothing mysterious or complicated about it.

Some of what you've learned has resonated more deeply than other things. That's OK. Just remember to be like Bruce Lee—customize and internalize what works for you, and forget all the rest. But one thing I hope you'll choose to remember is my encouragement that you begin your public speaking journey, and you begin it now.

People on their deathbeds don't lament the fact that they tried too hard, that they took too many risks, or that they pursued too many dreams too vigorously. No one says, "Boy, I'm glad I played it safe," or "I sure am glad I never tried anything too risky!" Rather they say, "If only I could go back and do it again, I'd act more boldly. I'd take more chances. I wouldn't let fear stop me from attempting great things. I'd make more decisions based on love and optimism, and fewer decisions based on fear and worry."

MR. JORDAN'S MANY FAILURES

There's an old Nike commercial in which basketball legend Michael Jordan recounts his many failures:

> I've missed more than nine thousand shots in my career. I've lost almost three hundred games. Twenty-six times, I've been trusted to take the game-winning shot and missed. I've failed over, and over, and over again in my life. And that is why I succeed.

On the surface, the point of the ad is that to achieve great things you must endure great setbacks. But the underlying point, besides "Buy Nike," is that winners don't let the fear of failure keep them from trying, and they don't let temporary setbacks keep them from ultimate success.

Jordan didn't shy away from the chance to take his first game-winning shot because he might miss it and be embarrassed. And he didn't refuse to take another game-winning shot when he had collectively missed twenty-five.

Instead he got up time and again, training harder and smarter, working on areas that delivered the biggest payoff (no doubt FM-AC), and practicing as he intended to perform. Jordan learned from his mistakes and built on his strengths. He didn't give up and hide, worried he might fail again. Instead he made his own opportunities by insisting, whether it was in high school, college, or in the NBA, "Give me the ball, Coach. I can do it."

MR. ROOSEVELT'S AGELESS CALL

You've likely read or heard the following quote from Theodore Roosevelt many times, but I hope it speaks to your heart as powerfully now as it continues to speak to mine.

> It is not the critic who counts; not the man who points out how the strong man stumbles, or where the doer of deeds could have done them better. The credit belongs to the man who is actually in the arena, whose face is marred by dust and sweat and blood, who strives valiantly; who errs and comes short again and again; because there is not effort without error and shortcomings; but who does actually strive to do the deed; who knows the great enthusiasm, the great devotion,

who spends himself in a worthy cause, who at the best knows in the end the triumph of high achievement and who at the worst, if he fails, at least he fails while daring greatly. So that his place shall never be with those cold and timid souls who know neither victory nor defeat.

Imagine what a different life Michael Jordan would have led if he'd allowed the fear of failure to prevent him from pursuing great things. Even if he had tried and failed at everything—my goodness, what a more interesting and worthwhile life that would have been than the cold and timid alternative.

As I've argued throughout this book, you should expect to do well at everything you do. At this point, though you'll no doubt benefit from re-reading certain sections, you should have an excellent grasp of what it takes to be a successful public speaker. And with a little experience under your belt, you're certain to flourish and grow your stage self into something powerful and impressive.

If you're already putting the advice in this book to good use, thank you. Thank you from me for making its writing worthwhile. Thank you from your fellow citizens who are sure to benefit from all you have to share. And thank you from your future self for committing to grow in a very fruitful way.

Alternatively, if you've read this entire book without speaking, or at least scheduling a speaking opportunity, now is the time. Not next week, not tomorrow, not later today. Fire up your email, pick up your phone, visit someone in person; then pick an opportunity, sketch an outline, and commit to give a presentation within the next two weeks, *now.*

It doesn't matter if it's for one minute or one hour, on CPR or baking cookies, at work or the town hall. Commit to giving a presentation—any presentation—now. The commitment will give you a reason to implement all you're learning, the presentation will be an opportunity to grow, and you'll be *so* proud of yourself once it's complete.

If you sincerely can't think of any opportunities to speak, think harder. If you still can't think of anything, drink some coffee. Then re-read Chapter Nine. And if you're still at a loss, visit a Toastmasters club in your area.

TOASTMASTERS

Toastmasters is a wonderfully professional member-run organization that specializes in providing aspiring speakers a safe place to grow. Members meet on a regular schedule, complete a very reasonable series of progressively complex speaking assignments, and give one another high-quality, positive coaching in a quasi-formal environment. With regular rotation of the roles (General Evaluator, Time Keeper, Toastmaster), members also get a chance to develop their general leadership skill. And from my experience, the senior members are incredibly welcoming and eager to help newbies develop at their own pace.

At your first meeting you can simply observe, but I encourage you to volunteer to participate in their "Table Topics" exercise, where you'll be invited to give an impromptu two-minute talk on a topic randomly drawn from a hat. Those exercises always make me a little nervous, but that's why I love doing them! They're such a fantastic, low-stakes way to improve. If it would help, I've even prepared your opening and close for you:

Good morning/afternoon/evening—my name is [your name], and I'm going to give a brief presentation on [the random prompt]. [Answer the prompt by thinking out loud, elaborating on whatever comes to mind. If you see a way to organize your ideas into 2-3 main points, go ahead. But in any case, just be honest and answer the prompt.] That's my brief presentation on [whatever]. Thank you so much for your attention.

That's it! The two minutes will be up before you know it, your classmates will clap and smile, and bam—you'll have completed your first impromptu speech.

Don't worry at all about how well you'll do. Your peers will be aspiring speakers themselves, each at different stages of development, with different strengths and opportunities for improvement. But rest assured that they'll all know full well that speaking off the cuff isn't easy, and so they're sure to be extra supportive, and extra proud of you for giving it a shot.

If you're not near a Toastmasters club, start your own. Just put the word out online or in the local newspaper, and meet every other week during lunch. All the info you need is at Toastmasters.org.

Or if you prefer, go fully independent. Find others interested in growing as speakers, settle on a time and place to meet, and make it happen. Besides taking turns presenting and coaching one another along, you could even help one another customize and work through the Quick Wins, Stretch Assignments, and Show Time presentations in Chapter Nine. No excuses. Get out there and present.

A FITTING CLOSE

Above all, the point that I hope you'll take away is one I've said many times in many ways: the key to realizing your enormous potential as a speaker is simply having the courage to get up there and the commitment to improve. Remember the not-so-secret secret from Chapter One? In that spirit, I'll encourage you now, just as I've encouraged you throughout, to get your nose out of this book and in front of an audience.

The only difference is that now you have a clearer idea of how to actually do it.

Sketch outlines for "Your Story" and "Checkout Speech" and commit to a specific date you'll actually deliver them. *Do it now.* Not next week, not tomorrow, not later today, but right now. It shouldn't take more than sixty seconds, and no matter your level of experience, both of those exercises are completely doable. Or find that Toastmasters club. Or create your own. It'll be fun—promise.

As David Schwartz taught us, *action cures fear.* Don't just think about doing it—do it. Remember how much better Dale Carnegie said he felt once he took action toward his goals? You'll be amazed how something as simple as sketching an outline will transform worry and anxiety into excitement and anticipation.

Then, as soon as you're almost ready—but not when you're completely ready, (because that time will never come, remember?)—schedule the presentation that prompted you to study public speaking. Once you've done it, reflect on what went well, what didn't, and dream bigger. Then bigger.

Roosevelt's extra nudge is a fitting close. Both a great man and great speaker, he mustered the courage to do many things most people go out of their way to avoid. And when he suffered setbacks, it only strengthened his resolve and bolstered his wisdom.

Unless reincarnation is true, this short life is the only one you and I have. Let's not spend a moment more on the sidelines. Focus where it matters and act where it counts. Act on those dreams before you feel you're fully ready. Put all you've learned in this book into practice…*now!* Do it for your public speaking coach. Do it for Tron Dareing. *Do it for you!*

Matt

For instructional videos and other public speaking resources, please visit

www.BestPublicSpeakingBook.com

And for information on Dr. Deaton's various projects and products

www.MattDeaton.com

Made in the USA
Middletown, DE
28 March 2018